LEADER
ZEN

Jess Stuart

ISBN   978-0-9951425-5-8   (soft cover)

ISBN   978-0-9951425-6-5   (Kindle)

Other books by Jess Stuart:

A Rough Guide to a Smooth Life (2015)	9781504343817
Like a Girl (2018)	9781973983460
The Superwoman Survival Guide (2020)	9780473517908
I Love Mondays (2021)	9780995142503
Burnout to Brilliance (2022)	9780995142527

CONTENTS

INTRODUCTION

After a few years of disruption, it seems like a chance to stabilise and rebuild. Yet we're still struggling to strike the balance with hybrid working, our teams are less engaged, burnout is on the rise and the economic impacts of the last few years are causing concern.

The last three years of the COVID-19 pandemic have taken a significant toll on the physical and mental health of workforces around the world. Supporting employee wellbeing and leadership development has become a priority for many companies.

According to Gallup's State of the Global Workplace 2022 Report: 'The pulse of the global workplace is low, but it's still beating.' This was the conclusion they drew from the following report findings:

- Global engagement and wellbeing trends are stable but low
- Employee stress is at an all-time high
- The global economy has lost trillions due to low engagement
- Before the pandemic, engagement and wellbeing were rising globally for nearly a decade – but now, they're stagnant.

More locally, at a 2022 webinar I ran with a large group of HR professionals, we shared the top challenges from multiple New Zealand based organisations, and there were some recurring themes:

- Retention of talent – head hunting
- Recruitment difficulties
- Talent shortage
- Employee burnout
- Engagement post-Covid-19
- Change fatigue, yet certain of more change
- Covid-19 hangover impacting people's wellbeing and resilience
- Budget cuts
- Leadership capability in this new era
- Time to lead and do more value-add impactful work over the noise and distractions
- Too many meetings; not enough thinking time or space
- Empathy burnout post-pandemic (too much caring for too long)

The recurring themes in multiple reports from across the globe are that pandemic impacts have affected minorities the most, and we're behind on our Diversity, Equity and Inclusion goals. We now see burnout being more prevalent in women than in men. According to a McKinsey study, we are also seeing an increase in microaggressions, particularly against women and more likely for those women with intersections of race, sexual orientation and disabilities.

Recurring themes have emerged from the work I do with leaders and their teams over the last two years. Most notably, we're struggling with constant change and uncertainty, long Covid and health problems, grief (missed family events, overseas isolation), guilt, resentment, burnout, hybrid working challenges, connection, collaboration, motivation, fear, division, overwhelm and disruption. Quite simply put, everything has seemed harder, due to the prolonged nature of the temporary fixes associated with the pandemic.

Over two-thirds of companies in the United States report having seen indications of employee burnout during the pandemic. Globally, access to safety nets and services for mental health lags significantly behind safety nets and services for physical health, at a time when the demand has never been higher.

As well as the Covid-19 implications we've also got economic impacts. This is especially true for our labour market and associated challenges, with smaller talent pools, higher salary expectations, and greater turnover as key staff members are headhunted. There's also a staff shortage caused by longer recruitment times and Covid-19-related absence. Some leaders have been in a position of having to deliver news of a pay freeze to staff who've gone above and beyond to keep the company afloat during the pandemic.

In the wake of Covid-19, employees across Asia Pacific are rethinking their lives, and work is topping the list. The PwC Global Workforce Hopes and Fears Survey 2022 of nearly 18,000 workers across Asia Pacific indicates the Great Resignation is set to continue. Talent is on the move to a degree not seen before. Thousands of expats have left the region and many locals have returned home. Millions of workers have quit or changed jobs. Employees say they want more meaningful work, a better deal around fair pay, and to be able to bring their authentic selves to work. But are their leaders listening?

- Only 57 per cent of employees in Asia Pacific are satisfied with their job.
- One-third plan to ask for a raise in the next 12 months and one-third plan to ask for a promotion.
- One in five intend to switch to a new employer.

These results should be a wake-up call for companies across the region, many of whom have already been grappling with a skill and talent shortage for years.

CHALLENGES OF HYBRID WORKING

We know hybrid working is here to stay but we also know it's not working for everyone. Whilst some have delighted in the newfound flexibility and lack of commute, organisations are now starting to observe the negative effects that working from home has on company culture, connection and engagement. Sixty-five per cent of employers say it has been challenging to maintain morale, and more than one-third are facing difficulties with company culture and worker productivity, according to a survey by the Society for Human Resource Management (SHRM).

According to Harvard Business Review, "The complexity of managing a hybrid workforce will drive some employers to require a return to the office."

More than half (53 per cent) of workers in a recent Gallup poll said they were looking for jobs that have more security than they currently have. The report suggests workers prioritise their happiness and wellbeing more now than they did before the pandemic.

It is clear leaders will need to adapt and evolve – at speed – to meet rising employee expectations for fair pay, meaningful work, authenticity and trust in a hybrid world. We expect new leaders with new skill sets and mindsets to emerge. Organisations that thrive in the future will select and nurture these leaders and invest in leadership training and development.

Leadership has been evolving for the last decade and the pandemic has seen yet another iteration as we keep up with the ongoing demands of the role. A shift from a traditional style of leadership to embrace leading a new generation and a post-pandemic workforce requires leaders who are authentic, calm, empathetic and collaborative. Leaders who have compassion, patience and the ability to listen; those not afraid to be vulnerable.

With strong awareness, they are adaptable, and capable of leading others through change whilst regulating their own emotions.

Common traits seen in old style of leadership	Traits required for this new era of leadership
Do as I say	What do you think
Follow my opinion	Follow my example
I know best	Inclusive
Indestructible	Vulnerable
Assertive	Considered
Hours worked	Value and impact
Control	Collaborative
Egocentric	Authentic
Crazy busy	Calm
Feared	Respected
Frustrated	Compassionate
Self-righteous	Empathetic
Reactive	Patient
Lectures	Listens
Rigid	Adaptable
Ignorance	Awareness

This book is designed to equip leaders to lead in this post pandemic era, and learn the skills required to lead in a way that prepares us for the future; to develop the traits associated with new era leadership. This book is broken into three parts, all based on Zen theory and made relevant for leaders: Knowing self, Leading self and Mind mastery.

First, we need to know ourselves before we can lead ourselves, and that of course comes before we can lead others effectively. We'll start by uncovering the secrets to self mastery with practical exercises that'll help you increase your awareness and become a conscious leader. We'll also look at strategies that'll help you better get to know yourself and your leadership brand. This includes the roles that authenticity, kindness and compassion play in leadership, and what we can learn from Zen traditions and decades of research in this space.

We'll then look at how we lead ourselves with executive stamina, resilience and energy to keep on top of the demands of leadership, including managing the unrelenting change and uncertainty.

We'll also explore the concept of mental fitness; something Zen monks are famous for, and a more Western term for mind mastery. How do we create space in the mind, remain curious, and master the art of equanimity, to stay patient and calm amid the chaos? How do we beat burnout and remain productive even during the busy times, so we're adding value and impact, and not getting distracted by noise?

Let's start by explaining what a Zen leader is, and how leaders can benefit from some of the ancient teachings of Zen traditions.

WHAT IS A ZEN LEADER AND WHY IS IT IMPORTANT?

"We are at an inflection point for leaders. But meeting the challenges of navigating the new normal isn't just about looking out; it's about looking in. What's missing from our conversation is how leaders need to show up ready to lead from what is best, wisest, more creative and empathetic in them."
— Adrianna Huffington, Huffington Post

Whether it's talent shortages, recruitment difficulties, performance management, engagement, or staff morale, leaders carry a heavy burden which has been exacerbated by the global pandemic – battling with empathy fatigue, change weariness, integrating hybrid working and trying to keep a culture of collaboration. It's no wonder burnout is on the rise as we not only adapt to a new normal but also lead others through this landscape.

LeaderZEN is a theory and associated practical programme that equips leaders to:

- Leverage self mastery and awareness as core leadership skills
- Develop an ability to adapt to change effortlessly and bounce back from setbacks
- Increase focus and concentration and access a flow state to enhance productivity
- Become fearless but wise, compassionate and respected

- Be empathic, with the ability to regulate and control emotional response
- Be an energised sustainable resource with the ability to innovate
- Embrace trust and presence of mind to guide decision making and conflict resolution
- Develop mental fitness and perform at your peak

Develop the kind of calm that is contagious – when you speak, others listen. As a conscious leader, you know who you are and stand in your power; cognisant and composed to navigate the challenges ahead and make an impact.

This is a new kind of leadership for a new kind of era. Post-pandemic challenges have changed the face of how we work and lead. It requires evolution and a new focus as leaders to ensure we're ahead of the curve.

LeaderZEN is for leaders who want to go:

From feeling this	To this
Spread too thin	Spacious
Overwhelmed	Calm
Scattered	Focused
Frustrated	Patient
Busy	Resilient
Exhausted	Energised
Reactive	Responsive
Competing priorities	Clear
Trying to be all things	Authentic
Full of dread	Positive

Despite how it's often depicted in the magazines, Zen is not all about being calm, although that'll be a side effect and a huge bonus. It's about increasing our focus and cognitive function. It's about self mastery and leading yourself, cultivating a mind that'll perform at its peak, being innovative and clear. It's also about the kind of leader you want to be in the world, that will add value and leave a positive impact. It takes courage and discipline and is not to be underestimated.

Many organisations I work with have a commitment to support their leaders to develop. They also have a goal to improve leadership capability and know this is an ever-changing and challenging role. The reason this is so important to organisations is because leadership impacts everything else that happens, both internally and externally.

Whether it's turnover, recruitment, conflict, engagement, staff morale, accidents, absence, employee wellbeing, diversity and inclusion, belonging, performance, or employer brand, all of this is impacted positively or negatively by our leadership. And of course, this in turn impacts the bottom line and our profit in the same way.

In *The 7 Hidden Reasons Employees Leave*, Leigh Branham says 89 per cent of bosses believe employees quit because they want more money, but in fact only 12 per cent of employees leave for this reason. Most commonly, people don't leave a job, they leave a leader.

A Careerbuilder.com study showed 58 per cent of managers said they didn't receive management training. Most of us get promoted for being technically good at our jobs – the one we might have trained all our life for. We inherit a team, but when it comes to leading, so few of us have spent adequate time training for this.

Let me ask you, who's the best leader you've had and why? What were the skills and traits they had?

They'll likely be competent in their job – that's why you respect them – but there'll be much more to it than that. In my workshops, common themes that emerge when asking this question include: *Empathy, recognition, support, challenge, integrity, communication, calm, authentic, trust. They communicated so I knew what was happening and what they expected. They listened and valued my opinion. They didn't micromanage me but trusted me to get the job done my way. They had my back. They helped me grow and develop. They cared about me as a person.*

It goes without saying, then, that a great leader will as a result of these traits have a highly engaged team around them.

Global studies reveal 79 per cent of people who quit their job cite lack of appreciation as their reason for leaving.

I spent a decade working as a senior leader myself in a capacity that allowed me to work closely alongside many other leaders. I was in Human Resources specialising in Leadership Development across multiple industries and countries, and I got to work alongside many different leaders. I saw what worked, and what didn't, and went on to spend another decade coaching leaders. It's a privilege to coach and run programmes for many different organisations. As a result, I get to see behind the scenes of so many different leadership journeys and company cultures, and there are some recurring themes.

When I left my HR career and started writing books, I was lucky enough to spend a year traveling the world with Buddhist monks and nuns, staying in ashrams and monastic communities along the way. These included Thich Nhat Hanh's Plum Village in France, teaching English to novice monks in northern Thailand, and visiting the Himalayan Kingdom of Bhutan. Whilst there's no denying that Zen theory is deeply founded in Buddhism (and other traditions) I've never considered myself religious. I do, however, have many life lessons this important time in my life gave me, and a passion to weave this ancient eastern wisdom with my modern people-psychology background of HR.

I believe there's so much we can learn from other cultures, and post-pandemic, leadership has never been so demanding. It seems like the perfect time to share this wisdom in a way that'll help leaders thrive and lead us through this period of change.

My passion is seeing people achieve their potential and it's a mantra I've applied to my own career too. From my own leadership experience, and that of the hundreds of clients I've worked closely with, there are so many barriers to this being a reality.

Back-to-back meetings, Zoom fatigue, changing priorities, managing poor performance or feeling like there's little support. Keeping up with the workload and still finding time to get the big stuff done. Caring for and supporting the team whilst also expecting them to deliver, and if we're honest, feeling a little bit of empathy fatigue since the pandemic. Distracted by the noise and the urgent work that keeps coming, yet trying to carve out time for strategic thinking and innovation. Wanting to inspire and motivate others but struggling to find the energy to do this even for ourselves. Feeling worn down and less tolerant, in a way that make Zen and calm seem like a big ask. Dancing on the edge of burnout but clinging on to the treadmill in a bid to keep going and prove you can do it.

The Covid-19 pandemic took a huge toll on our leadership. Not only were we going through this ourselves – supporting our families, home schooling our kids, getting sick, and worrying about the future – we were also responsible for carrying our teams through this. Trying to provide leadership and direction when there was no playbook, and no one really had any idea what was happening. Job security and change were concerns on everyone's mind and none of us could guarantee we'd not be impacted. Add to that economic concerns and it was a tough landscape to lead others through. There's also the feeling of achievement many of us find is lacking as we come up for air post pandemic. Having spent the last 2-3 years surviving Covid-19 and keeping the doors open in the office, BAU (Business as Usual) was parked and all the things we wanted to achieve had to take a back seat. It leaves us with this feeling of being behind. Or like we've not achieved anything, even though surviving the last three years and keeping a team together has been an achievement all of its own.

Leadership starts with us, which is why we'll first focus on self mastery. It's a big step in the right direction. We'll explore the concept of mental fitness and sustainability to ensure we keep ourselves in the best shape possible to lead others through this landscape. We'll also look at the Zen aspects of emotional regulation and equanimity. What would it be like to remain calm and patient regardless of what was happening around us? An essential skill in this new normal as we deal with teams who've lost their tolerance, feel change fatigued, and are scared about the future while simultaneously grieving for the past.

If you like the sound of self mastery and want to:

- Be a leader that is calm, clear, focused and capable.
- Master the art of equanimity and learn how to make space to innovate and create.
- Understand how to navigate the new normal and lead others through this challenging landscape.
- Be able to respond rather than react in the heat of the moment.
- Manage hybrid working and keep your team engaged to reduce the overwhelm and perform at your peak.

Come on this journey with me as we learn the Zen art of Leadership.

SELF MASTERY: LEADERSHIP STARTS WITH YOU

"Knowing others is intelligence. Knowing yourself is true wisdom. Mastering others is strength. Mastering yourself is true power." – Lao Tzu

The secret to achieving your potential is to first know yourself. This means connecting to your values, knowing who you are and what you bring to the table; understanding your strengths and limitations and unpicking some of your limiting beliefs. Once you have the awareness, you must then have the confidence and self-efficacy in who you are and what you stand for. This is standing in your power and leading authentically, which we'll talk more about.

Once we have mastered self-knowledge, we need the energy to deliver on what we know we're capable of, and this is the other side of the coin: leading ourselves.

We often think about leadership as something we do to, and for, others, yet it always starts with us. Without this deep understanding of ourselves we cannot be effective leaders or lead with confidence. This plays into our performance, our resilience, and of course, our energy.

That brings me to this concept of self mastery and probably the centre pin of the Zen view. Whether it's martial arts or meditation, the Zen masters have a deep intimate knowledge of themselves, and the utmost self-control as a result.

When we have mastered ourselves, the rest is easy, but mastering ourselves is one of the hardest things to achieve.

When we have developed self mastery, we move forward consciously and steadily towards our goals. We know our purpose, and we have the self-discipline needed to do things in an intentional, focused way. Self mastery also means mastering our emotions, impulses, and actions, and is vital in terms of leadership brand.

Think about people you know who don't have any self-mastery. They're probably impulsive and might let their emotions control them. They're unpredictable and, as a result, people are less likely to trust them.

The kind of skills we associate with self mastery include much of what we'll go on to talk about in this book; self-awareness, discipline, emotional intelligence, positive thinking and equanimity are key elements.

A conscious leader is aware not just of themselves, but also of others and their environment. Conscious leaders are awake to opportunities; they can read a room and they often know what's going on before anyone has spoken a word. This deep awareness gives them an advantage and is achieved through self mastery.

The best ways to build awareness are through reflective practices and gathering feedback. Practising awareness is also a key aspect of mindfulness and presence, which we will cover in later chapters.

What have you done to learn about yourself on your leadership journey so far? Probably a personality test which would have put you in a box based on stereotypical norms. Perhaps a 360-degree appraisal which will have given you an insight into what others think, and can be useful as a starting point. For self mastery we must go beyond the basics though.

Let's get practical and start to learn more about ourselves. We can't just talk about self mastery without doing the work. Some of you might be further along on this journey, in which case these exercises will be easy. For others, it'll provide a valuable starting point on this path of self-discovery. We'll look at our strengths and values as well as internal parts of ourselves, and how all this contributes to make up our leadership brand.

KNOW YOUR STRENGTHS

Gallup surveys have found that if we focus on our strengths, we'll be six times more likely to be engaged at work, eight per cent more productive, and three times more likely to have an excellent quality of life. It's no wonder, given their data, they advocate for a strengths-based approach to leadership development.

Strengths are important, yet we often ignore them in favour of talking about what we need to work on or improve, where our leadership development is concerned.

As a nation, we tend to err on the side of modesty. We can find it difficult or embarrassing to accept compliments; we are conditioned to be modest and not to promote our abilities, through fear of being seen as arrogant.

Strengths can also be quite tricky because they feel effortless. If we're good at something, we tend to find it easy, so we assume it's nothing special, that everyone must find it this easy.

We are predisposed to focus on the things we're not good at, rather than the things we are. It's how we've evolved and have used to keep us safe. We're constantly scanning the horizon for the worst that can happen, so we are able to react and prepare for that, which helped us survive back in the days of sabre-tooth tigers. However, in our modern life, this translates to noticing all the things we don't like about ourselves, the things we've not done yet, and where other leaders are performing better.

We're also very quick to move on to the next thing in our modern world and so don't spend time reflecting on the positive – what went well, why, and what strengths we used. It's about rewiring the neural pathways in our brain to see things more evenly. It's not that life will be any different; we'll just learn to see more of the positive as well as the negative.

Life has evolved at an amazing pace, and we've not caught up. Dr Barbara Fredrickson did some research on 'positivity ratios' and found to offset this bias that exists in the brain, we need a ratio of 3:1. That's three positive thoughts, emotions or experiences to every one negative.

There's a lot of work to be done in this space, as our negativity bias is like a well-worn walking track; we use it often. To even this out, we need to start firing more of the positive neural pathways and breaking down a less-travelled path in the brain. It's bumpy and overgrown with weeds, and so much more difficult to navigate.

It takes time, like training a muscle. We don't go into the gym and pick up the heaviest weight, and this is similar. It's not an overnight thing; we start small and build up – it takes practice.

Research has proven that focusing on our strengths makes us more successful, but first, we need to know what they are.

Stop for a minute and write down a list of your strengths – all the things you're good at. What feedback have you received? What did they tell you they'd miss about you when you left your last team?

My top five strengths are:

1.

2.

3.

4.

5.

Others tell me my strengths are:

1. ....

2. ....

3. ....

4. ....

5. ....

VALUES AND BRAND

Alongside our strengths, our values are an important aspect that determines our brand. When we live by our values, there is a sense of internal rightness and fulfilment. The best way to determine our values is by looking at what we actually do. We also discover our values by exploring what we care deeply about – what makes us tick. It is generally these things that provide the why behind what we do. It's our essence and who we are at our core, regardless of who is watching.

What are your values? I remember when I was first asked this question. I didn't even know what values were; I had to Google a list and then start picking out words that resonated. Now I have card decks of values that I use with leaders and teams, to do this similar exercise. It's a powerful way of becoming more self-aware, but it's also a powerful way of connecting teams through shared values.

Find a list if it helps get you started. Pick ten that apply and then narrow that down to your top five. Our values drive the decisions we make and the way we lead.

Once we know our strengths and our values, we are on the way to articulating our leadership brand. Our brand is what people know us for – our reputation. It's how we demonstrate our credibility and become known for who we are and what we stand for. It's something that's created whether we are intentional about it or not. Based on our actions and behaviour, our brand already exists, and will be known across our teams and colleagues without us intentionally having set out to create it.

We are all unique. Part of leveraging our own uniqueness is to understand what we bring to the table, how others perceive us, and what we want to be known for.

When building your brand goals, ask yourself the following questions:

- What are my natural strengths?
- What do I do extremely well?
- What do people acknowledge me for?
- How do I add value at work?

Beyond our strengths and values, there's a third part of this puzzle in understanding who we are, and that's based on our experience both at work and, most importantly, in life. There will be meaning that we've created and lessons that we've learned from some of the biggest experiences we've had across our lifetime.

TIMELINE EXERCISE

When I became a thought leader, I invested in my own development at business school, and one of the exercises I found useful was this idea of charting your timeline. This is a way of understanding who you are and how you've been shaped. If you were to chart your life on a timeline, what key moments stick out? Life events, relationships, trauma, transformation? What jobs did you have and what did they teach you? Start right from your first job as a teenager through to now.

- What big moments happened in your life – what did you learn?
- What are your proudest achievements?
- What are your top successes?

being born   **present**

Once we start thinking about the experiences we've had, and what we've gained and learned from them, it starts to become apparent why we do what we do or feel the way we feel. We discover the things that are important to us and the skills we've developed as a result of our experience. We've all got different sides to ourselves – it's what makes humans so fascinating, and on this journey of self-discovery, we start to put more pieces of the puzzle together.

A system of self-knowledge that I've used for both myself and clients is based on the model of Internal Family Systems (IFS), created by Richard Schwartz. It is a systems-thinking approach to psychotherapy that identifies and addresses multiple sub-personalities or families within us.

According to the IFS model, parts of our personalities often play four common roles:

1. Managers: protective parts that function to control people's surroundings and manage emotions and tasks to navigate daily life.
2. Exiles: parts that hold hurt, fear, or shame from early experiences, and they carry the difficult emotions and memories associated with those experiences.
3. Firefighters: activated in times of overwhelm and pain.

Firefighters aim to inhibit those difficult emotions by any means necessary, such as substance use or binge eating.

4. Self: a genuine self, waiting to be accessed. The Self can identify, observe, and help the other parts become less extreme, be more productive, and coexist effectively. The Self has many positive traits, including confidence, calm, creativity, clarity, compassion and courage.

I like to think of it as the voices of the noisy neighbours that live in our heads, and the different parts of us that show up at certain times and have certain influences, all with their pros and cons. Schwartz also points out these are just parts of ourselves, and there are no bad parts, but increasing our awareness helps understand our behaviours and how to play to the positive sides of these traits.

What are your common traits and do they fit into categories you can name? I love playing with this, and seeing what we come up with when we name these parts ourselves. Here's an example below (it's actually my four selves) and then space for you to create your own. You decide on the name for each of these characters, and it's often helpful to consult those who know you well, to add to some of the traits that show up when that particular character is at the wheel in your brain.

EXAMPLE

Name	Monk (Self)	Name	Winner (Exile)
Traits	Patient, calm, compassionate, thoughtful, wise, self-aware, reflective, quiet, creative	Traits	Driven, ambitious, resilient, takes risks, stubborn, compares to others, competitive

Name	Avoider (Firefighter)	Name	Goody two shoes (Manager)
Traits	Stops communicating, Procrastinates, lazy, prefers the easy way, eats and sleeps more	Traits	Loyal, sensitive, studious, has integrity, people pleaser, plays it safe

MY FOUR SELVES

Name		Name	
Traits		Traits	
Name		Name	
Traits		Traits	

You might find it useful, once you've got your four selves outlined, to ask these questions:

- How do these selves play out for me and impact my behaviour?
- What are the light and dark side of each self?
- Where do some of my beliefs or early influences play out here?

When we know ourselves, we align to our purpose and gain more of a sense of meaning in what we do. What we're talking about here, when we pull all of this together, is purpose. Which, in Buddhism and other Zen traditions, is often called Dharma or Dhamma. Simon Sinek called it our 'Why' and the Japanese model of Ikigai is famous for it too.

Dharma is our unique purpose in life. It is the process by which we use our unique skills and passions to serve our community and the world.

The word dharma is an ancient Sanskrit word. It's not just about what we do, but how we do it, and why we do it. Our dharma is not a career, or a project, or a certain role we play. It's the unique core of our being that our soul carries to everything we do and every way we are.

It's often referred to as our inner compass or true North. It's living in accordance with who we fundamentally are, leading authentically, knowing what makes us tick, and what we bring to the world.

Self mastery is not to be confused with confidence. Just because we think we're great or have it figured out doesn't mean it's true. In fact, it's more likely to indicate we've not mastered ourselves at all, and is a common theme among narcissists.

Self mastery is to be aware of our strengths and limitations and to be self-disciplined to work on ourselves and grow, with the self-control to exert a strong will against our impulses and to steer our inner ship with equanimity.

It's a commitment to never-ending improvement; it's a process of becoming. This journey of self mastery requires us to find ways to transcend fear and break through resistance.

I spent 10 days in silence doing this, having undertaken a couple of Vipassana meditation retreats. This requires you to stick to a strict, monk-like schedule which involves meditating for approximately 10 hours a day, taking a strict moral code (called precepts), and adopting a daily routine much like monks and nuns. To sit with uncomfortable thoughts and feelings when you're without distractions for that long helps gain insights into who you are and what you want to be.

Self mastery isn't about controlling ourselves or dominating those fearful parts within us. It's about getting to know these parts, and then transcending them. That is why it's such a challenge, because on the one hand we have the drive for growth, and on the other hand a need for safety, so these two psychological needs can often compete in this space. We stop when it gets hard or want to run when the fear arises, and yet it's an inevitable part of our growth.

For those familiar with Carol Dweck's work on Growth and Fixed mindset – a growth mindset is critical to this path of self mastery. This theme of continuous learning, and embracing the vulnerability that comes with it, is not always an easy path.

According to Deepak Chopra, to be focused on the path of self mastery requires us to be one-pointed without being rigid. It requires us to stay alert, unemotional, and mature. To be firm without oppression, to be resolved without judgment, to be strong with humility. It requires us to practise silence and stillness so our inner wisdom can reveal itself. Self mastery also requires us to be courageous; to step out from the crowd.

My advice is always to take it slowly. Self mastery can take years, so patience is a must. Always ask yourself "what have I learned from this?" Take small steps along the path by setting small goals. Go easy on yourself and know we're all a work in progress and this doesn't stop us also being a masterpiece at the same time.

What does your personal development plan look like? In my experience, as leaders, we often spend a lot of time working on these for our team and direct reports, but not the same amount of effort and accountability on our own. Don't wait for someone to ask, sit down and write yours now.

What's your vision for your future self? What kind of leader are you, and who do you want to be?

Once we know who we are and have begun this journey towards self mastery it becomes so much easier to embrace authenticity, and to do so with the confidence that the skills, experience and essence we bring to our roles is enough.

Over the last decade we've talked a lot more about kindness, compassion and authenticity in leadership. Words previously never associated with great leadership are now seen as core skills. These are also key elements and foundations of Zen practices.

LEAD LIKE YOU LIVE: AUTHENTICITY

"True belonging doesn't require us to change who we are, it requires us to be who we are." – Brené Brown

I love the concept of leading like you live. When we've grown to the point of self mastery, this becomes effortless. It is who we are, regardless of where we are and the role we find ourselves in. It is congruent and authentic and allows a human-centred leadership that means we're bringing our whole selves to work.

When I first entered management, in a male-dominated timber manufacturing business in the UK, I used to think showing any signs of kindness would be viewed as weak. I used to play down skills like empathy and try to act like the tough business leader I thought the world expected me to be.

Authenticity wasn't talked about then, certainly not in leadership. I used to feel like I took my 'Jess' hat off at the door and put my leadership hat on, which was a sort of armour based on who I thought a leader should be. None of it was authentically me, but I was desperate to fit the mould and had no other experience to draw from.

I now run "Lead with Confidence" programmes for emerging leaders, and when we start a new cohort there are always people waiting to be told the secrets, given the key to the secret leadership box and learn a whole heap of new skills they didn't know, in order to be 'a leader'. It makes sense, as that's how we prepared for our technical roles, often for decades. Learning what we needed to know and becoming qualified before we got the job. Leadership tends to happen the other way around and most of us learn by doing. It's true though, that most of the unique skills and traits we've had since school are the same ones we end up relying on when we get into leadership.

My mentor and leadership expert, Matt Church, often says it's a predisposition not a position, and I think this is so true. It's a way of being, not a title – something we are, not what we do.

When we are authentic, we:

- Are true to our own personality, values, and essence (regardless of any pressure to act otherwise)
- Are honest with ourselves and with others
- Take responsibility for our mistakes
- Align our values, ideals, and actions

Back in my manufacturing days, when I was a senior leader, we constantly had a focus on Health and Safety, but despite the rules and procedures to keep people safe, there would still be accidents. We had what we called the '3 am rule'. If you were on night shift and no one else was around at 3 am, what would you do? Would you wear the PPE (personal protective equipment), take an extra five minutes to do it safely, or cut the corners because no one is looking? It's like wearing steel cap boots in the factory, but chopping trees with a chainsaw in your back garden barefoot. It's who you are that determines how you do things, especially when no-one is watching.

The self mastery chapter will have given you a great starting point in this journey, but it's likely you'll also have come up against some resistance.

Because we're human, there will be a tendency to think that it's not enough, or to look at other leaders and compare. Let's look at some of the challenges to us being our authentic selves.

The biggest two, in my experience, are comparison and perfection. Even when we know who we are, we sometimes wish we were a little bit better, or more like that person.

Brené Brown explains this beautifully: "Comparison is the crush of conformity from one side and competition from the other. It is trying to simultaneously fit in and stand out. It says be like everyone else but better."

As humans, we are predisposed to compare to others. There is sometimes this feeling that the grass might be greener on the other side, or that we'd be better leaders if we were more like them.

Interestingly enough, science has found that the way the angle of grass is viewed does affect how green it appears, and when viewed from afar it is greener, which I think is a metaphor worth remembering here. When we compare to others and covet their skills, we never know what we're trading in that comparison. Perhaps they have internal anxiety; poor relationships because they work too hard; their name on the door, but a lonely home to go back to, and they might even envy aspects of your leadership style.

I'm a big believer in the grass being greener where we water it, and for self mastery, we can only be ourselves. It is so much easier (and more rewarding) to embrace the potential within us than to wish we had the potential of others. The bottom line is we all have potential, we all have strengths and weaknesses and we're all different.

We also have ideas of what a leader should be doing or saying in certain circumstances, and the image we've built up in our head of the things we 'should' be as a leader.

Of course, a lot of this comes from a need to belong and fit in. "I should do this because everyone else does it." It's a recipe for comparison and perfection.

Do you ever find yourself falling into the comparison trap –

that you should be more, better, further along? I used to, often, and occasionally still do! Especially after scrolling through social media looking at what everyone else is doing and how successful they seem to be.

When Dr Libby Weaver was in town, I went to her weekend event, and we exchanged books and chatted a little. She has written 13 books in 13 years, and apparently it takes her about a month per book! I've always admired her kindness, her passion, how she relates to her audience and how she's built her business. She's always there at the start of her events, stacking books and greeting people, and again at the end.

Now, the old me may well have fallen into the comparison trap: "It takes me six months per book, I'm only on my fourth one, I could never fill a room with a thousand people despite the fact that I live here."

This time, as I admired Dr Libby and all she's achieved, I was left feeling inspired, not falling short. If she can create this in 13 years, just imagine what the next decade can hold for me. She's much further down this path than I am, and I can learn so much from people like her.

It takes time to build up a business and a following, which is why a sell-out tour across multiple countries takes more than a few years and a couple of books. We all have to start somewhere, and it's from that point we grow, at different speeds and in different directions.

Admire others and allow them to inspire you with their achievements, but don't compare yourself to someone else's journey. So often this leaves us feeling like we're falling short and takes us away from what we've achieved so far.

When we compare ourselves to others, especially the famous, successful ones, we end up feeling like we're not enough. My wife famously told me that despite being a successful leader she worried her mum wouldn't be proud of her when she realised Jacinda

Ardern was her age and had just taken up office as the Prime Minister!

It can be our comparison to others that encourages us to aim for perfection. A common trait in high achievers, it often comes from our fear of failing or making a mistake. Yet as humans, that's an inevitable part of us learning and growing. The drive for perfection often comes from an insecurity based on not being good enough. We're trying to prove ourselves, and over deliver when we aim for perfection. It's understanding the difference between excellence or mastery and that additional, unrealistic step, perfection. Perfection wants to deliver above and beyond excellence and mastery, and we know that doesn't always exist. Which is why so often when we aim for perfect, we set ourselves up to fail.

Yet perfection is often held up as the standard we should aspire to, and a positive trait in leaders. My experience is that it actually puts us at higher risk of burnout, micromanaging and never feeling like we've achieved enough. It's also less authentic and so can detract from our self mastery efforts. Dame Jenny Shipley said, at a conference I was at one year, "The closer you are to perfect the less people will trust you." It really stuck with me. In an era where we prize human-centred leadership and authenticity, appearing superhuman or not real in some way means people are less likely to feel we're genuine. They're less likely to build trust and connect with us as a leader. When we're authentic and congruent, and vulnerable about our imperfections, it's so much easier to trust and connect to because people can see it's real. It's a fundamental component of human-centred leadership.

When we show up as human, we're more genuine; people trust us and can see we have integrity. There's a congruence that comes with authenticity. Whilst vulnerability is hard, it becomes an advantage in the leadership space when building an authentic brand.

To complete our section on self mastery I'd like to discuss two popular Zen ideas and much talked about leadership skills. They're also skills we've commonly left out of the workplace, yet research suggests they have huge benefits for leaders. If these are skills you naturally possess, embracing them will help you become a more authentic leader.

COMPASSION & KINDNESS

"People will forget what you said. People will forget what you did. But people will never forget how you made them feel." – *Maya Angelou*

Compassion is taught in most Zen traditions and is vital for our own happiness. When I think about compassion, I'm thinking about kindness to yourself and others. When we're compassionate, we come from a place of love. But how does this relate to leadership?

Richard Carlson speaks of compassion in his book *Don't' Sweat the Small Stuff,* saying it helps us build our perspective towards others. The willingness to empathise, recognise their problems (which are often worse than our own), opens our hearts and enhances our sense of gratitude. Wouldn't the world be a different place if we were all a little more compassionate?

Vietnamese Zen monk Thich Nhat Hanh said, "The word 'compassion' is a verb". Just think back to the last time you performed the action of helping someone in need. How good did you feel?

Our natural response to seeing someone in distress is the impulse to help; we care about the suffering of others, and we feel good when that suffering is released. This applies whether we do it ourselves, see it in a movie or witness it in real life. It makes us feel good. Feeling like we're making a difference in the world and helping those who need it brings us joy; it gives us meaning.

James Baraz quotes statistics on why giving is good for you in his book, *Awakening Joy.* "According to the measures of Social

Capital Community Benchmark survey those who gave were 42 per cent more likely to be happy than those who didn't. Psychologists even have a term for the state of euphoria reported by those who volunteer, it's called 'helpers high' and is based on the theory that neuroscience is now backing up. Giving produces endorphins in the brain that make us feel good, this activates the same part of the brain as receiving rewards or experiencing pleasure does."

Buddhists say, "All the happiness there is in the world comes from us wishing others to be happy." When we do good deeds for others it makes us feel good. Our "compassion" bank is as important as our financial bank. We need to make regular deposits so we have savings, otherwise we cannot withdraw from it when times are tough.

Compassion is more likely to make us kind, and kindness in leadership is something we've heard a lot more about in the last decade.

Harvard Business School's Amy Cuddy says that even before establishing their own credibility and competence, leaders who project warmth are more effective than people who lead with toughness. Kindness and warmth appear to accelerate trust. But, the link between kindness and great leadership extends beyond just the relationship we have with employees. Studies show it also increases employee performance.

Leaders who are influential in modelling kindness to their staff benefit from increased employee wellbeing and engagement. Kind leaders create environments where relationships thrive, and people feel safe. This includes self-respect, respect for others, respect for diversity and the value it brings. Psychological safety is a key outcome of kindness in leadership.

A question I often ask at my workshops is, 'What do you admire most in others?' The top answer is often kindness, usually followed by calmness and confidence.

Kindness is a skill that has been underrated for too long – in fact, it was once seen as a weakness in the workplace – but we're now starting to understand its strength and value.

For many years, particularly in business, I'd been led to believe kindness was a weakness. People would say, "If you're too soft, you'll be walked all over. You need to be tough." However, I've learned over the years that kindness is a strength – one that's crucial to our success in business and life. We can be kind and still be strong and not get walked all over.

Former Prime Minister Jacinda Ardern said: "One of the criticisms I've faced over the years is I'm not aggressive enough, or maybe somehow, because I'm empathetic, it means I'm weak. I totally rebel against that. I refuse to believe that you cannot be both compassionate and strong."

Most of us are brought up today to look after number one, to go out and get what we want, and the more of it we can have, the better. Our society preaches survival of the fittest and often encourages us to succeed at the expense of others.

I was no different, and while I noticed a tendency to feel sorry for others, and wanted to help, I was too busy lining my own pockets and chasing my success to act on these impulses. I worried that kindness was me being soft and was therefore a weakness that might hamper my progress, especially at work, as I progressed up the career ladder.

In more recent years, I've noticed that making time to be kind builds trust and relationships, and garners the sort of respect that leads to strength in a leader, and this is what I teach others.

Don't get me wrong – it is not about being lenient, giving in, or not holding people to account. It's about being reasonable, fair, open and trusting, supporting others, empathising, recognising them when they've done well and showing you care.

2021 research by Signature Consultants, an IT and professional staffing provider, uncovered a clear connection between the practice of kind leadership and a company's ability to create an environment which facilitates and supports innovation. In fact, according to their Humankindex Study of U.S. workers, leading with kindness is the most effective leadership style to drive innovation and competitive advantage in the marketplace.

It's too easy to justify desire, self-indulgence and miserliness with the survival-of-the-fittest mentality. We tell ourselves this is based on Darwinian evolution and competition to survive.

What we have overlooked is that a fundamental part of our survival is cooperation, working together, and looking after each other. Humans did not evolve to be big and strong or have big fangs; we survived because we helped each other.

Kindness increases our sense of fulfilment and joy, it helps us build resilience, and it is also a source of strength, as well as a skill that aids our success.

Often linked to kindness and compassion, empathy is another much talked about leadership skill. Let's talk about Emotional Intelligence, which of course includes empathy.

EMOTIONAL INTELLIGENCE

When I was growing up, the emphasis was all on IQ (intelligence quotient, or cognitive intelligence). The cleverer we were, the better job we'd get, the higher we'd climb the ladder and the more successful we'd become. I'd worked for over a decade before I even knew what emotional intelligence was.

Daniel Goleman's book on the subject opened my eyes to its power and put the pieces together in a way that made sense for me. Goleman cites studies showing as much as 80 per cent of the average person's success, in both personal life and career, can be attributed to our level of emotional intelligence. This means as little as 20 per cent of a person's success is a result of IQ.

It makes sense: if we're strong in empathy, we are more likely to get along with our fellow humans, and if we have control over emotions, our relationships will be more effective. We'll also be better able to read the room, influence, and negotiate with this kind of awareness.

Emotional intelligence is the ability to understand and effectively manage our emotions. People who have high degrees of emotional intelligence can better manage emotions, insecurities or fear, and are therefore able to react to many situations in more appropriate and effective ways.

US psychologists, Drs John D. Mayer and Peter Salovey, published the first formal definition of emotional intelligence in 1990. They have also described emotional intelligence as being "knowledge of self and others" and, more specifically, "the ability to monitor one's own and others' feelings and emotions, to discriminate amongst them and to use this information to guide one's thinking."

Goleman says those with emotional intelligence have the ability to motivate themselves, persist in the face of setbacks, manage frustration, control impulses, regulate mood and keep distress from swamping their ability to think. They are also strong in empathy and hope. If it sounds familiar, it's because we're talking about self mastery here.

In my 15 years in human resources, I have worked with many business leaders and seen how emotional intelligence contributes to great leadership, as well as how critical it can be to success in relationship-building, communication, and influencing and managing a team.

Emotional intelligence is now seen to be one of the must-have leadership skills and those with high levels of EQ seemed to have done a better job of leading their teams and countries through the pandemic. It helps us with empathy, resilience, people skills, relationship management and communication. It's our motivation in the face of setbacks, the ability to understand and manage ourselves and others, it's the awareness we have of both ourselves and others, it's our passion, and it's our ability to make good decisions.

According to the 2021 Ernst & Young's Empathy in Business Survey, 90 per cent of U.S. workers say empathetic leadership leads to higher job satisfaction, and 79 per cent agree it decreases employee turnover. Kindness and empathy are key to employee engagement.

So, we've explored self mastery, along with some practical exercises to help us get to know ourselves better. We now have a good idea of our leadership brand and why leading authentically is an important part of LeaderZEN. We've learned the importance of reflection and feedback to build self-awareness, as well as the idea of bringing our whole selves to work and leading like we live.

Once we know ourselves, the next step is to lead ourselves. This means sustaining our energy, building resilience, and gaining executive stamina to respond to the demands of leadership.

EXECUTIVE STAMINA: LEADING YOURSELF

"Almost everything will work again if you unplug it for a few minutes, including you." – Anne Lamott

For me this is another foundation of not just our leadership success but our life too. We're only able to deliver on our potential if we have the energy to do so, and in a world of busyness and stress this seems more challenging than ever.

So many leaders I meet are exhausted and not able to find time to reenergise. Whether it's workload or family commitments, we always put something else ahead of our own resilience and the result so often is burnout and an impact on performance, tolerance and capability.

It's like the WOF and service on our car – if we don't look after it and get the scheduled maintenance, it doesn't function as well.

Rituals and routines are common in Zen practices and often our self-care is a series of habits and rituals we either prioritise or not. It's how we build executive stamina and have the reserves to draw from for the demands of leadership.

Part of the reason, I think, that leaders perhaps don't take this as seriously as they should is the name. Self-care makes me think of green juice, incense and yoga studios and whilst that might be your self-care ritual, it doesn't work for everyone. It can come across as a nice to have, a luxury item, a reward or an indulgence; something seen on Instagram, and less important than everything else you have to do today.

It's why it got a rebrand in leadership programmes to 'Executive Stamina', despite the fact we're talking about the same thing – what we do to keep us functioning at our best both mentally and physically.

For me, we're actually talking about performance here rather than wellness (although wellness is a positive side effect). It changes the language in a way our organisations understand. Wellness has long been a focus, and aside from a few lunchtime meditation classes, free fruit in the staff room, and some resilience training, we've not shifted the dial.

When I look to the sporting world, they have perfected this approach. Their approach to performance is that peaks must be followed by troughs of rest and recovery. Massage, saunas, days off and rest actually feature as part of their jobs and their performance schedules. Pre-match preparation and post-match recovery are integral parts of ensuring peak performance. Athletes see it as a non-negotiable that their energy, shape, and physical and mental health are directly linked to their success. So why hasn't this translated into our organisations?

I believe it's about changing the conversation from one of self-care to one of performance.

It's why I now talk about sustainability. It's a popular term when we talk business sustainability, or about the environment and climate change. Yet we don't use the word in association with ourselves. We are our most important resource, so it makes sense to ensure we're also a sustainable resource. I believe our energy and condition is a direct predictor of our success. Ensuring we're a sustainable resource, and our teams are too, is one of the foundations of success and peak performance.

For too long we've seen self-care as a nice to have, a luxury item and a bit of an indulgence, rather than the key to sustainability and a critical pathway towards peak performance. It's why so many of us feel guilty for prioritising it, or that it's something we can go without if we're busy.

So what do you do to keep yourself sustainable? What does your employee sustainability policy look like? In my workshops, I often use the analogy of a road trip (in an EV of course, because we're sustainable). When we're on a long road trip and our fuel light comes on, we'd never dream of driving past a fuel station. We stop and pull over to refuel even though we know it'll add minutes onto our journey. We do this because it helps us get to our destination and without it, we're left broken down on the roadside. Yet how often does our inner fuel light come on and we push through, don't have time to stop and refuel; assume we can refuel when the work is done? The result? We don't get to our destination, our metaphorical vehicle doesn't perform as well as it could, and sometimes we're left broken down on the side of the road.

How do you know if your inner fuel light has come on? What are the signs to look out for?

I like to think of this in terms of traffic lights. We all have green and red zones, and they look different for us all.

The red light stops us completely; it's our ground zero. The green light is when we're at our best. The amber light, in between, is important because it's our warning system. When we slip from green, before we hit red, the amber light gives us an opportunity to act and pre-empt hitting the wall and slipping into the red zone.

For me, an amber light is a twitch in the corner of my eye, a sore throat and a constant tiredness. I start to forget things and I notice I'm less tolerant and a bit snappy with loved ones. This is my amber light; my warning to back off, take a rest and pre-empt the approaching red zone.

So, what do these traffic lights look like for you? What do you notice about yourself when you're at your best, on green? What about when you're at your worst and close to burnout, on red? And the bit in between: what are the early warning signs you get at the amber light? This stuff is your inner fuel light coming on.

	When I'm in the green zone I
	When I'm in the amber zone I
	When I'm in the red zone I

All Blacks' mental skills coach, Gilbert Enoka, talks about this in terms of performance waves. Waves come in sets. For the All Blacks, the peak of the wave should be game day, when they push hard, compete and perform. But, Enoka says, this always needs to be followed by recovery time, a rest day: the calm water or trough before the next wave. Trying to perform at the peak of the wave all the time simply isn't sustainable. To get to the peak, we must also experience the trough: in fact, it's the troughs that prepare us for the peaks. As a surfer, I know how much energy it takes to paddle out, catch a wave and surf it in. We can't spend the whole session doing this. We need the troughs in between waves to recover.

It's a concept I refer to as 'slowing down to speed up'. I know it sounds counterintuitive, but bear with me.

If we slow down by taking small pauses in our day to recharge and press reset, we'll be more effective when we return to our day. If we are clear-headed and well rested, we function better. We get things done more quickly, navigate setbacks with ease and have more space to innovate. All of this together means by slowing down, we are in fact speeding up, by becoming more effective, sharper and performing at our peak.

The hour I take on a lunch break means my afternoon workload of 5 hours now only takes me 3. I've gained an hour by spending an hour refuelling. It means I'll make fewer mistakes and be more effective. I can make decisions more accurately and solve problems easily with a sharp, focused, refreshed mind.

For me, sustainability is our resilience, it's our energy to be our best and our ability to bounce back from the tough times. I believe building resilience is the best way to ensure we're sustainable, as well as forming sensible habits around work-life balance and how we use our time.

Resilient leaders can motivate themselves in the face of setbacks; they are optimistic, they learn from their mistakes, solve problems, and look for solutions. They have self-control and are not afraid to seek assistance from others. It's important though to make this doable. With our busy schedules, not only do we have to prioritise it, but find the time and space to fit it in.

If we don't prioritise this, the effect will be something like when our phone battery dies before we can get to the charger: we've overused it, and not given the batteries time to refill. We'd never dream of taking our mobile phone out of the house without a charger if it had low battery, yet we do it to ourselves all the time. Running around on empty, without taking the time to recharge, and then expecting that we still function well. The beauty of this practical tool is that we can do it anywhere and it takes very little time. An energy audit allows us to see where we're at, and then we know what we need.

If, like your mobile phone, you had a battery indicator displayed on you right now, what would it say? It's a simple tool of an energy audit that tells us where our energy levels are and if we're in need of a recharge. To take this one step further, what activities or experiences in your life help contribute to charging that battery, and what drains it? Again, this gives us an insight into managing our own energy levels and responding accordingly.

What sustains me?	What drains me?

I use self-care as the foundation from which I build. If I feel good and have plenty of energy, everything else seems so much easier, even when the tough times hit.

As a solopreneur, I see self-care as part of my job. If I go down, my whole business does.

I love a massage once a month – for me it's a non-negotiable, not a luxury item. I see it as part of preparing for my work, like the Olympians you see getting massages before and after events. It's not for pleasure, but so they can perform. I view this as the same for me, just with a lot less running!

Self-care is not in any of our job descriptions, but I think it should be. Maybe then we'd take it more seriously? Or at least we'd feel like we had permission to prioritise it, in the same way we do our workload. If you're a leader, it's your job to be at your best, to manage your energy and know what you need. You'll only be capable of leading others if you first lead yourself.

Self-care looks different for everyone. It doesn't have to cost money, take lots of time, or be difficult. In fact, it should be the opposite – it should make life easier.

What do you do to keep yourself recharged and sustainable? Is it enough? When do you do it, and how do you make the time for it?

Given the demands on our time and the world we lead in, this has never been more necessary. Yet the fact is we're still busy and can struggle for time. Let's explore how busyness and burnout play a role.

BUSY AND BURNED OUT OR PRODUCTIVE AND EFFECTIVE?

"Productivity is less about what you do with your time and more about how you run your mind." – Robin Sharma

Busyness is at epidemic levels in our lives and our organisations. Are you busy or effective? It's an interesting question, because most of us have been conditioned to believe the busier we are, the more productive we'll be.

We all want to be productive at work, and for many organisations, productivity programmes have been all the rage over the last couple of decades. It's not just about increasing what we produce though and the output as productivity suggests, it's also the quality of the output – how effective we are.

We live in a world that prioritises quantity over quality – more is always better. The more hours we work, the more valued we are as an employee, the more successful we'll be, and the more we'll earn – it's where the hourly rate came from.

Since the industrial revolution we've measured performance in a way that suggests more is better – the harder we work the more valuable we are.

I'd like us to flip the narrative on this and understand that more is not necessarily better, especially where performance is concerned. We can work hard, but only to a point. Without the necessary balance, the hard work starts to become ineffective. It's less about how much we do and more about the value we add, and this is the difference between quality and quantity.

We hit a point at peak performance where further quantity starts to impact on the quality of what we produce. This is the time we're more likely to make mistakes, less likely to innovate and less tolerant with those we're working with. At this point, more quantity starts to decrease our effectiveness until we eventually hit burnout.

We're also less compassionate and equanimous when we're overstretched and busy. The 1973 Good Samaritan Experiment 'From Jerusalem to Jericho' had students prepare short talks about what it meant to be a minister. Some of them were given the parable of the Good Samaritan to help them prepare. (In this parable, Jesus told of a traveller who stopped to help a man in need when nobody else would). Then some excuse was made for the students to switch to a different room. On the way to the new room, an actor, looking like he needed help, leaned in a doorway. Whether a student had been given material about the Good Samaritan made no difference to whether the student stopped to help. The researchers found that if students were in a hurry, they were much less likely to help, and on several occasions, a seminary student going to give their talk on the parable of the Good Samaritan literally stepped over the victim as they hurried past.

If we can do enough to hit peak performance without doing too much or losing our effectiveness, we've hit the sweet spot.

The more we do in a day, the less we'll do well, if it's coupled with a sense of overwhelm and exhaustion. As a result, we can't be at our best.

It's this difference between quantity and quality, and being busy or effective – they don't mean the same thing. In fact, the busier we are, the chances are the less effective we're going to be.

The bottom line is, as leaders, it's not the amount we do but the impact we make, and that's more about value and quality.

As a leader, if there's too much on our radar and we've stretched our bandwidth, we can end up majoring in minor things. If we're busy, we're probably distracted by the noise and not able to focus on the priorities.

In fact, busyness not only detracts from our performance, it leads us closer to burnout, which we know has become a big issue, both around the leadership table and in our teams.

I wrote a whole book on this, *Burnout to Brilliance*, so we'll just scratch the surface, so you know what to look out for in yourself and those you lead, as well as how to avoid it.

The term 'burnout' was first coined in 1974 by Herbert Freudenberger, in his book, *Burnout: The High Cost of High Achievement*. He originally defined burnout as; 'The extinction of motivation or incentive, especially where one's devotion to a cause or relationship fails to produce the desired results.'

We use the term "burnout" to describe physical, mental and emotional exhaustion. It's more than the fatigue we experience at the end of a demanding week though. It's an exhaustion that doesn't ease up after a long weekend recharging the batteries.

According to a 2020 study by the Mental Health Foundation, a quarter of New Zealand adults are at risk of struggling with their mental health.

The World Health Organisation predicts burnout will be a global pandemic in less than a decade, and the World Economic Forum estimates an annual burnout cost of GBP 225B to the global economy. We know there's an organisational cost of burnout too, with increased turnover, absenteeism, and of course, the obvious impact on performance.

Burnout is not just about quantity but the quality of what we're doing, not just how much of it we're doing.

According to *Psychology Today;* Burnout is not simply a result of working long hours or juggling too many tasks, though both these play a role. The cynicism, depression, and lethargy that are characteristic of burnout most often occur when a person is not in control of how a job is carried out, or if they are asked to complete tasks that conflict with their sense of self.

The most common indicators that burnout is at play are; exhaustion, a feeling of lack of control, disengaging, trouble focusing, a sense of dread about work and frequent feelings of cynicism or irritability.

From my book, *Burnout to Brilliance,* here is the "Five Stages of Burnout" reference table, charting the degree of seriousness as we move from stage one to five.

5	Loss of hope, withdrawal, detachment, illness, depression
4	Checked out, discontent, loss of motivation, noncommitment, exhausted
3	Frustrated, lack of results, resenting others, feelings of guilt, anxiety, not coping, struggle sleeping
2	Overwhelm, lack of focus, working long hours
1	Loss of energy, too busy to take breaks

If we're tired, burned out, and not at our best, everything else drops on the gauge too, not just our energy. It decreases our resilience, our confidence and our ability to focus. It impacts our tolerance levels, and our ability to bounce back from setbacks, or make decisions and come up with great ideas.

Our cognitive function declines, disrupting creativity, problem solving, and lowering emotional intelligence. It also negatively impacts our memory, concentration, attention, and just about everything we need to be great leaders. It's an experience that's familiar to me and may be to you too.

My burnout came in my early thirties and at the height of my corporate career. I'd just taken over covering the role of a colleague in addition to my own. Now heading up two teams and looking after 10 sites instead of five, I was stretched further across the country, sitting in more leadership meetings and involved in more projects than I could keep up with.

I spent most days in the car or in back-to-back meetings. I had little time to enjoy the beach house I had settled in, as I was always away working, staying in hotels. When I was at home, I had little time or energy to indulge in any hobbies or exercise, or even function in my relationship. But the high achiever in me kept pushing. More was better: I had to prove myself, and failure was not an option. Besides, I didn't want to let people down. Of course, this was before I'd discovered Buddhism or Zen monks.

My boss at the time called me to ask if I'd manage a big change project about to hit the manufacturing part of the business. I was going through a breakup with my partner of seven years, and she thought it might 'help take my mind off it'. It was the straw that broke the camel's back.

When I think back, the signs were there. It was a slow burn; it was just always more convenient for me not to notice. I was always on the verge of getting sick, battling a tiredness no amount of sleep or long weekends could cure. My batteries always seemed to be running on empty, and I'd lost my motivation for practically everything. I didn't have any joy in my work, or in the things I used to enjoy in life. I withdrew from friends, as I hadn't the energy to socialise. I justified it by telling them how big and important my job was, and in my own head told myself I needed the rest and that senior leaders couldn't be expected to socialise during the week; it wasn't part of the deal. In hindsight I can see I was checking out, losing motivation and ultimately disengaging from work and life because of my burnout.

It was this experience that helped me put executive stamina front and centre for my energy and how I show up. Rather than a nice to have or a luxury indulgence, this now became just as important as any business activity because it fuelled all of the business I did and had a massive say in the impact that I was able to produce. It ensured that I had the resilience to keep up with leading and the wisdom to know what aspects to prioritise amid the busyness and noise.

It's easier said than done though, and quite often with this it's not that we don't know what to do – we just don't get around to doing it.

I ruptured my cruciate ligament playing soccer many years ago and since then, surgeries and physiotherapy have been part of my rehabilitation. At a recent review the physiotherapist gave me just two exercises. She said she didn't give people any more because they simply don't do them. It got me thinking about setting realistic expectations and setting ourselves up for success. She'd made it achievable, and it worked – I remembered what they were, and I've been doing them.

So often as high achievers we want to do it all and do it all perfectly and if we can't, we feel we've failed. But what if we just focused on the basics and made it more achievable? Especially where sustainability is concerned.

Some days I have time to do yoga, meditate, go for a walk and prepare nutritious food. Other days the only thing I can do is go to bed early and drink plenty of water.

I like to think of it as having a Plan A and a Plan B for my self-care routine. Plan A is always the preference and yet it's the hardest to stick to when times get busy. If we can't do Plan A we often end up doing nothing and then feel bad. What if there is a Plan B to fall back on? A mini, doable version of Plan A for those busy days.

If I've got the time, my Plan A is a yoga class, meditation before I leave the house, a walk with the dog at lunchtime, and bed before 10 pm. On the days I'm up early for a flight, speaking at a conference and then at the conference party that night, the Plan B is a meditation app on the flight, and some stretches before bed.

Plan B is a mini, less time-consuming version of Plan A, so is ideal for those times we get busy and feel like we don't have time for self-care. And most importantly, it's a way of still ensuring we can do the stuff that matters, recharge our batteries and take care of ourselves.

I believe in the 80:20 rule (if we do this stuff 80 per cent of the time, the 20 per cent we miss because life gets busy is inconsequential). If all we get to do is a week of Plan B because it's busy, it's still better than nothing and will have a positive impact on our health and wellbeing.

So, what's your Plan A and Plan B version of self-care for your own sustainability?

It's the power of rituals, and many would say in particular our morning routine. It's how we start the day that sets the tone for the rest of how the day may play out. I know what it's like when I sleep in and get behind before I've even begun. Nothing goes as well as when I enter the day with a bit more calm, purpose and organisation.

Often our morning is the place we can get the most space. It's something we have control over and is moveable, depending on what time we want to get up. It's why Robin Sharma's 5 am Club became such a popular movement. As a former monk he was well versed in the value of an early start and rituals. What does he suggest we do after getting up at 5 am? 20 minutes intense exercise, 20 minutes reflecting on your goals and 20 minutes learning a new skill – all Zen concepts that monks build their practice on.

Of course, if we're getting up at 5 am we also have to go to bed early, and sleep is another predictor of success when it comes to sustainability. It has been said that our morning rituals actually begin before we get up, and how we sleep will impact how the day starts too.

Oprah Winfrey, Robin Sharma, Deepak Chopra, Tony Robbins, and Bill Gates all have been in the 5 am club.

You don't have to get up at 5 am but the principle is valid. Carve out an hour or two of space in your morning to be purposeful and intentional about your day and set it off to the best start. It also cures all the excuses for why we don't get time to do the things that keep us sustainable and invest in our executive stamina, because now we've got an hour or two every morning if we get up early enough.

It's often quiet, still and peaceful early in the morning when everyone else is sleeping. There are fewer distractions, and it gives us the kind of space that just doesn't exist at any other part of the day. My friend Lisa says she feels like she's the first to have discovered an island and she's the only one there when she gets up at 5 am.

Former Twitter CEO Jack Dorsey's daily wellness habits include fasting, five-mile walks, and two hours of meditation per day. Dorsey wakes up at 5 am every morning. His morning ritual includes a 60-minute meditation and an ice bath.

Indra Nooyi, former CEO of PepsiCo, had a morning routine that has inspired several other CEOs to follow suit. Her early wake up time helps her orient her day to achieve more.

Sundar Pichai, CEO of Google Alphabet, also likes to wake up early, at around 6.30 am, so he can follow a set routine. His morning tea, breakfast, and physical newspaper have been a core part of his morning for decades now.

The recurring themes from the many well-known CEOs who openly talk about how they keep up with the pace is the support they have, the way they prioritise their own sustainability and the benefit of a routine to achieve this. Their routines commonly include similar elements too. All speak of exercise and moving the body, as well as exercising the mind, whether it's with meditation, reflection, learning or solitude. These, along with sleep and nutrition, are common features.

Of course, building our stamina and remaining sustainable is not just about all the things we do. It's just as much about the things we don't do, and this can be pivotal. In fact, if we're busy leaders struggling to find space, this could well be the answer. Saying no and setting good boundaries.

In *Atlas of the Heart*, Brené Brown quotes writer and coach Prentis Hemphill: "Boundaries are the distance at which I can love you and me simultaneously." I think that's beautiful, and so true. So why do we struggle to set boundaries or feel guilty for sticking to them?

At my recent retreat we were talking about boundaries and how, particularly for women, saying no can be difficult. We feel guilty or selfish, as if we're letting people down. In addition, we've often been brought up to be obliging and put the needs of others before ourselves. It can lead to us burning out, feeling resentful and being last on our own list.

For those who've burned out, you know we're no good to anyone and can't give to anybody else if we don't first look after ourselves. It's the notion of putting on your own oxygen mask on first, or not trying to pour from an empty cup, that we hear so often as analogies in this space.

We get told we just need to 'learn to say no' and set better boundaries, but that doesn't stop the feeling of guilt, or pressure (and expectation) we get externally to break our own boundaries for the sake of others.

For many, saying no is easier said than done, and only once we've made the mindset shift can we say no and set boundaries with ease, without the guilt, and with the knowledge it's best for everyone.

And it's this simple equation that gets us there. It's not what I'm saying no to, but what saying no actually means; because in reality when we say no to one thing, we are saying yes to everything else:

Saying no to working late is saying yes to my family.

- Saying no to other people's emergencies means I'm saying yes to the important deadlines I have on my own schedule.

- Saying no to an extra project because I'm overloaded means I'm saying yes to my health, energy and the quality of what I'm delivering.

- Saying no to a party after a full week of work means I'm saying yes to myself and avoiding burnout.

So, by setting boundaries, it's not what I'm saying no to, it's what I'm saying yes to. When we focus on what we're saying yes to, the boundaries become much easier to put in place. We're leading with our priorities and focusing on what's important. Reframing the 'no' from a negative into a positive.

It can be quite impactful in terms of giving us permission to say no by focusing on what we're actually saying yes to. Remember; when I say no to this I'm saying yes to everything else.

Our resilience and stamina are key to unlocking peak performance and keeping up with the pace. They keep burnout at bay and are also fundamental in helping us navigate change and uncertainty, which have become constant over the past few years. The added responsibility as leaders means it's not just ourselves we have to navigate through this landscape; we must lead our teams through the change and uncertainty as well. Many Buddhist texts and Zen traditions talk much about the nature of change and how nothing ever stays the same. It is the law of nature and yet so often something we struggle with in our organisations. Let's learn how this ancient wisdom can support our change management.

MANAGING CHANGE AND UNCERTAINTY

"In nature it's not the strongest, most intelligent that succeeds it's those that are most adaptable to change." – Charles Darwin

A central focus in all things Zen is the law of nature; the impermanence of all things, and that change is part of life. Wouldn't it be easy to perform at our peak if everything went to plan and everyone just left us alone to get on with our job?

Change is a constant, nothing stays the same. Yet when change happens, we can be resistant. We like certainty, we like structure and routine, and when changes happen (particularly when they're not of our choosing) it can throw us off course. Our need to cling to the familiar and certain is often the very reason we struggle to adapt to change.

This has never been truer than during the Covid-19 pandemic and resulting lockdowns. Weddings were cancelled, big family events missed, families separated, and ways of working and travelling changed forever. We had fears for our health, our job security and for many, the grief of a temporary loss of freedom.

There's so much we can learn from ancient traditions that translates into our modern lives, particularly on this topic.

I've learned that in the face of change, it's not what happens to us but how we react to it, and that we have a choice. This has been instrumental in changing the way I respond to challenges. So much of what happens we can't control, and this can leave us feeling helpless like victims. When we focus on what we can control, we become empowered, and this is where we get to choose.

Sometimes we can't change our circumstances – the only thing we can change is our perspective.

As humans we spend so much time trying to avoid suffering, and chase after the good feelings. We want life to be good all the time and are uncomfortable sitting with sadness and suffering. It's why addiction is so prevalent; we attempt to numb the suffering and replace it with a 'high', whether from food, drugs, alcohol, work, or something else.

We chase after the highs in our life (the perfect job, house, partner) and when we get one of them, we cling to it and hope it never leaves. Likewise, when we feel sad, we desperately want it to pass and to feel happy again. Whoever we are, there will be a mixture of good and bad in our life. We all have challenges; the good news is they don't last. These feelings we want to avoid don't last – but nor do the good ones. Everything comes and goes; this is the nature of life.

This is epitomised by the story of a novice monk who would often complain to his teacher, "I've been working on this all week and I'm struggling to get it." The teacher responded with "It'll pass." Delighted the following week, the novice monk runs up to his teacher and says, "Teacher, I've mastered it", to which his teacher responds, "It'll pass."

Everything that comes, also goes. It is the law of nature and truth of life. Like the tides of the ocean that come and go, the day that always turns into night and then back again, and, of course, the seasons. If you're like me you'll wish summer lasted forever yet we know it's always going to turn to winter – which doesn't last either, thankfully.

But whilst suffering is inevitable, misery is not. Accepting the things we can't change allows us to make peace and move on. Good and bad will always come and go – sit with what is and accept what we can't change.

Central to Buddhist teachings are the concepts of *acceptance* and *impermanence*. Everything will come and go whether we like it or not. None of us will live forever, everything we have we can lose. It's why attachment in Buddhist teachings is deemed the root of suffering.

One thing we all know for sure is we will die, there's no greater certainty, yet we live like we'll live forever and it's an utter surprise to us when we lose someone we love; we're completely unprepared.

Think of it like staying in a five-star hotel on a luxury island. We know we're only there for a short time so we make the most of the fine white sheets, the fluffy bath robe and the beautiful food. We enjoy it and appreciate it, but we don't believe we'll take any of it with us, or cry when we leave, because we knew right from the start we'd be checking out.

This doesn't detract from the pain these transitions cause us though, and the hurt of grief and loss.

None of us like to suffer and yet it's inevitable; it can also be where our biggest lessons come from. During my time at Plum Village, Thich Nhat Hanh's place in France, I read his famous book *No Mud, No Lotus: The Art of Transforming Suffering.* In fact, I now have a lotus tattooed on my foot as a result of the impact of this important lesson.

The lotus is a beautiful flower that grows from the mud. We too grow from our challenges to bloom into the beautiful humans we are. It's because of the mud we become a lotus and without the mud we wouldn't bloom. Suffering is part of the human condition and it's OK not to be OK. If we get sick or lose someone we love, of course we'll suffer, but sitting in the mud is often how we get through those times, and over time the lotus starts to bloom. Sometimes our deepest scars can lead to our biggest gifts.

It doesn't stop us going through the grieving cycle though and this applies to any loss, not just the big ones. Anytime something changes, we are losing what we knew and adapting to the unknown. It's a transition we go through, and a process that the Kübler-Ross Change Curve model captures perfectly.

Whenever we enter into a change not of our choosing, it's common for us to go through this process. It's a model I used in my HR days when we talked about restructures and redundancies and the likely response people experience when entering such an uncertain time. It's useful to know what kind of emotions we –and others – will experience, so we can navigate through this process and understand its impacts.

When we first learn of a change, whether to our job, a redundancy, a relationship breakup, or even, on the smaller end of the scale, a new system or a new boss, we can find ourselves in a state of shock as we adjust to the prospect of things changing. It's not uncommon to feel denial; "This can't be happening to me, I don't want to face this yet or think about what it could mean."

This is followed by a range of emotions that leave us feeling anxious, frustrated and sometimes in despair (or depression, as Kübler-Ross refers to it on the curve). We can find ourselves thinking; "What does this mean? What will I do now? I wish this wasn't happening".

We all take different amounts of time to navigate this curve and it's not always linear. We can find ourselves going up and down it; back and forth as we figure out what's happening and process our emotions. One minute we think we've made our way through the anger and feel sad, and then all of a sudden, we're back at anger again. None of this is unusual.

Then we start to enter the upward curve into the positive; the more future-focused feelings. We've had time to process the change and we begin to experiment with possibilities; "Maybe this could work, here's what I might do." We then make a decision to accept this is happening and finally, integrate it into our new normal. At this point we've accepted the change and are ready to move on.

The impact as we navigate this curve, of course, is on our motivation, our mood, and our performance that changes over time. The more time we have to adjust, the easier it becomes, and the more likely we are to get to a place of acceptance and transition to the new normal – until it all changes again of course.

This has been true of Covid-19 lockdowns. One minute everything is normal, and the next, the kids are home and you're not allowed out. With no certainty on when that'll end either. We go through a range of emotions and feel the impacts until eventually we adjust and adapt, even if we still don't like it. Then of course, the lockdown ends, and we start the curve again with the new change that is our reintegration into society!

This is why resilience is so important; it's the ability to bounce back from setbacks and respond to change.

If you've heard me talk about this, you'll know I'm an advocate for this being a constant focus, not just when we need it. It's too late at that point. It's how we balance the drive to do more with those troughs between the waves I mentioned earlier. I liken it to a bank account we pay into over time; so we can withdraw funds when we need to – when the tough times hit.

It's easy to be happy when everything is going well, but we know that's not always the case, and that's why we should all have a focus on building our resilience and looking after ourselves. Because tough times come to us all at some point.

A tree grows its roots when the weather is fine so when the storms come, it stays standing strong. If we wait until we need resilience to start building it, we'll find we'll be trying to grow roots in the midst of a storm.

Regardless of who we work for and what job we have, we will come across people who frustrate us, people who underperform, and people who think and act differently to us. We'll also likely be involved in restructures, or even redundancies, and have to leave a job, or adapt to a change not of our own choice.

What this Zen theory of impermanence and the law of nature allows for is an acceptance that change will come, and a preparedness that then comes with that. It also allows us to appreciate what we have, knowing it's not going to last forever. The art of acceptance and the ability to appreciate are other key elements of Zen customs and integral not just to good leadership but a happy life.

The ability to be grateful is often overlooked, yet for enhancing our awareness it's one of the best things we can do. It cultivates a more positive mind, and it helps bring us back to the present. Both are necessary elements of building awareness and mindset.

UCLA neuroscience researcher Alex Korb (*The Upward Spiral*) has revealed that the most important question to ask when we don't feel our best is, "What am I grateful for?" The impact this has on our brain trains it to be in a more positive place.

The antidepressant Wellbutrin boosts the neurotransmitter dopamine; so does gratitude. Prozac boosts the neurotransmitter serotonin; so does gratitude. Even if life is hard and we can't think of anything we've got to be grateful for that day, it doesn't matter. Studies show it's the searching that counts – this has the uplifting impact on the brain.

A study from the University of Pennsylvania shows that when leaders are grateful to their employees, the employees are 50 per cent more successful.

Studies found that leaders who express appreciation are more influential, respected, and happier. In a Glassdoor survey, 81 per cent of employees said they would work harder for a grateful boss.

Best of all, positive recognition is contagious. So, it may also be the case that gratitude makes us better leaders.

Expressions of gratitude are not just feel-good gestures – they actively energise and motivate.

Gratitude is also an important individual quality for leaders to cultivate in themselves. One reason that being thankful improves self-control and decision-making is that it is connected to humility. Both gratitude and humility are integral to emotional intelligence, which is an essential leadership quality and key to self mastery.

Gratitude is something that is easy to practise, yet so easy that we underestimate its impact. Try it for 10 days and see what it does for you. At the end of each week, I have a planning meeting with myself. On the agenda are successes from the last week, what I need to focus on for the week ahead, and three things I'm grateful for. It can be that simple.

We've discovered top tips for managing change and uncertainty, as well as how to build executive stamina and resilience in order to perform. This ensures that we don't just lead ourselves but can lead others too.

Part of our resilience and executive stamina is our mental fitness; in fact I'd say probably the biggest part. It seems so big that it didn't seem right to put it in the chapter on executive stamina. It's also linked to much of the self mastery wisdom we've discussed, so for that reason has a whole section of its own. I don't use the term 'life-changing' very often, and yet mind mastery can be exactly that. The third part of this model on mental fitness and mind mastery sits across everything else in this book and supports the other two sections we've discussed. It is the key to awareness, resilience, performance and mindset. It is so fundamental that we've saved the best for last – to me it's a skill that sets leaders apart. If we can master our own mind, everything else (in both work and in life) becomes so much easier. This includes our emotional regulation and equanimity, decision-making, problem solving, beating burnout, responding to challenge and how we learn. It enables creativity, awareness, focus and calm.

"Only when you can be extremely pliable and soft can you be extremely hard and strong." – Zen Proverb

MENTAL FITNESS: MAGNIFICENT MIND

"When you change the way you look at things the things you look at change."
– Wayne Dyer

For leaders this is huge, because our mind doesn't only affect how we function cognitively, but also how we feel about ourselves and everyone around us. It can change our perspective and regulate our emotions as well as allowing us to focus, make decisions and solve problems. Leadership of self is an inner game, and this is where it all starts. In the bid to lead ourselves and get good at self mastery it really does all begin in the mind.

First, we must understand how the mind works, become aware of our own thinking patterns, and then learn how to cultivate a clear, calm, peak performing mind, like a finely tuned instrument.

We hear a lot about mental fitness these days and we often refer to highly intelligent people as having a 'magnificent mind', but what does it really mean to have our mind cognitively functioning at its peak, and how does this impact what we're able to achieve?

A mind that performs at its best is one that is rested, clear and calm. It is one that can be present and focus and is therefore sharp and cognitively functioning at its peak. This is a magnificent mind.

A Magnificent Mind:

- Is sharp and quick
- Is aware
- Has space to create and innovate
- Is calm and quiet
- Knows what it wants
- Functions like a well-tuned instrument
- Helps us manage emotions
- Is more resilient
- Is clear
- Is a positive space
- Can focus and concentrate with ease
- Is a happy place

The mind is so powerful and plays such a crucial role in how we show up and how we experience life. The difference between the glass-half-empty and the glass-half-full people we know is the lens they view life through, and that starts in the mind.

The mind is something we cannot escape from, regardless of how much money we have, how far we travel or how popular we are. Our mind will always be there, and so will the thoughts we put in it, which is why it's essential to ensure those thoughts are positive, helpful ones.

We take our thoughts with us everywhere we go. If we're having unhappy thoughts, it doesn't matter if we're at a five-star tropical resort in the sun; we'll still feel unhappy. Or, as monk Matthieu Ricard puts it; "If you're having suicidal thoughts and someone gives you a luxury penthouse apartment, all you're going to do is look for a window from which to jump."

Much of the time, we don't even know what's happening in our minds – we're too busy to notice the chatter. We're not sure what it's up to and whether this is helpful for us or not.

Imagine if a megaphone broadcast all our thoughts for the duration of today – what impact would that have? We'd probably not have a job anymore, many friends left, or a relationship, by the end of the day!

Yet this stuff is going on in there all the time. We can have a barrage of negative self-talk happening in our minds and not even be aware of it.

Our minds are wired to think more negatively, so it is an uphill battle to try and train the mind to think more positively, yet it is key to helping build our resilience. Many major sports teams have tapped into the power of positive thinking, and many businesses now leverage the power of positive psychology.

After all, it all begins in the mind. What we think becomes how we feel, and that in turn becomes how we act and the results and outcomes we experience. This is why it's vital that our minds are positive and not negative places.

In our busy lives, we are often on autopilot. We get lost in the doing at the expense of being. Have you ever arrived at work and not remembered the commute? It's when we are focusing on other things and our minds have wandered that we are not paying attention, and life passes us by.

A 2010 *Harvard Business Review* article on multitasking found it is in fact a myth. When our brains are seemingly multitasking, what they're actually doing is switching from one thing to another in very quick succession, often within microseconds.

So, we must ask ourselves what quality we are giving these simultaneous thoughts when we're multitasking. If we can't actually do many things at once, are we doing them justice by trying to?

Multitasking has become ingrained in our culture, which is why the alternative of slowing down seems so counterintuitive. Gerald Weinberg explains, in his 1992 book on Systems Thinking, that frequent switching between tasks costs us on average as much as 40 per cent of our productivity.

In a world where multitasking is seen as a necessary skill, being mindful is the opposite. It is slowing down to focus on one thing at a time, one moment at a time; to give full concentration and unwavering attention to just one thing.

Our brains are so busy. One of the reasons we feel so overwhelmed is the amount of information rushing through our mind at any given time. The research varies: we have somewhere between 60,000 to 90,000 thoughts during the course of a day. Either way it's a lot to process and not surprising that we suffer with information overload.

When we think about how busy life has become, how much there is on our schedule and the expectations we place on ourselves, both at home and at work, it can be overwhelming. Sometimes the mind feels full of fog, with a million and one things buzzing around in there, without the space to think about any of them clearly.

The mind has always amazed me and in following a decade of studies in mindfulness across the world, I've come to understand the power of our mind, how we treat it, and the impact it has on everything we do.

The brain has 86 billion neurons, all capable of firing different neural pathways. The ones that fire together generally wire together but so often we're not conscious of just what those are. We are unaware of the quality of the well- worn pathways in our brains we're forming day after day, and the thinking patterns that are driving us.

The good news is that neuroplasticity means we can literally rewire those neural pathways and form new thought patterns, thus improving cognitive function.

One of the things I quickly learned when meditating is the power of watching our thoughts. Not just noticing them, but learning what was going on inside my head and stilling the tide to the point where I could create space. Space to think more thoughts, as it often turns out. But it is the mind's job to think, so it's not surprising this happens. It's not about stopping thoughts but allowing them to pass through, to settle, and subside.

We are not our thoughts, but they do have a massive impact on how we feel, and the outcomes we experience in our life. That's why it's so important to be in control of our thoughts, but it's also great news that they don't have to define us.

If I were to tell you, three years pre-Covid-19, there was a queue outside the supermarket, you'd think I was crazy. We certainly wouldn't go and stand in it; it just wasn't something we expected to do. But for a while it became the norm and something we all did without questioning.

I liken the thinking patterns in our mind to cultivating a garden. What we water grows, and that can be the beautiful flowers, or the weeds. If we water the weeds (negative thoughts) we end up with a mind full of weeds that are out of control, leaving no room for beautiful flowers to bloom.

What we focus on grows. So what kind of mindset are your thinking patterns cultivating?

This can certainly be true for stress. Stress is something we often think is caused by external circumstances. It's people or situations that stress us out. Yet in reality, stress is our response to something external. For example, a traffic jam is only stressful if you're running late. Someone else can be in the same jam and not be stressed. So, it's not about the jam, it's about our reaction to it. It's the same with our kids; they can act up one day and we'll let it slide, but if they do the same thing after a hard day at work followed by an argument with our spouse, we'll likely lose it. It's the same behaviour so it's not that causing the stress, it's our reaction and our response, based on how resilient we feel, how tired we are and what else is going on in our life. If it rains and I'm in the city without a raincoat, I find it stressful, but if I'm at home and the water tank is low it's anything but – same rain, different response. Stress is not because of an external object; the stress is caused by our internal response.

The good news about this is, if stress is an internal response, we can do something about it. We can't control the external circumstance, e.g. that thing my colleague just said, but we can control our response, and this is the part at which this becomes stressful or not.

Buddhists have a great analogy for this that sums up perfectly how attitude and mindset impact our resilience. It's called the 'second arrow' analogy.

If we're walking through the forest and we are hit by an arrow, we have a problem, and it causes us pain. Our reaction to this problem is like being hit by a second arrow in the same place. Now we have two problems and double the pain – the difference being the second arrow is one we shot ourselves.

It's not about what happens to us but how we react to it. The second arrow represents our reaction, getting upset and angry about the initial problem. For example, the car may have broken down, and we are inconvenienced. That is our first arrow and the resulting pain that's not of our doing. If we choose to get angry and upset about it, our reaction is the equivalent of shooting the second arrow. It will double our pain but do little to resolve the first problem, and we did it to ourselves.

So, what neurons do you fire together, and where are the well-worn tracks in your brain? What are they telling you about your mindset?

In his book *Think Like a Monk*, Jay Shetty describes two types of mind that I think we can all relate to, and something I think highlights this concept of a Zen mind well. We often function in the monkey mind (busy and overwhelmed) and our preference for peak performance of course is closer to the monk mind (calm and Zen). I've expanded on his theory to create a glimpse of these two minds.

The monkey mind is	The monk mind is
Overwhelmed	Calm
Fearful	Conscious
Negative	Positive
Blaming	Compassionate
Critical	Collaborative
Overthinking	Patient and disciplined
Procrastinating	Committed
Distracted	Focused
Self-centred	Self-controlled
Anxious	Solutions focused

In my experience, the two biggest differences I've made cognitively have been through stilling my mind, and being more present and aware. Both of these skills I've cultivated through regular meditation.

A mind that is still and aware can think more clearly, innovate, respond rather than react, and is also a more calm, pleasant place to be. It's easier for me to be a glass-half-full kind of person when I have an organised, clear, calm mind producing my thoughts. It's also easier to perform well if I can solve problems, make decisions and have a clear head. This also helps with focus and concentration, which we'll talk more about towards the end of this chapter. But first, how do we master our mindset and cultivate this calm and clarity?

When I titled this book and the subsequent programme, I didn't want them to be 'Mindfulness for Leaders' or to be viewed as meditation for managers, because it's so much more, and yet we can't talk about this stuff without also talking about the practice that links it all together. There's a reason why monks and Zen masters devote so much of their life to this ancient practice and spend so many hours a day meditating.

It's something that helps build awareness, keeps us in the present, builds resilience, lowers stress, and aids creativity and innovation. It's the way we cultivate equanimity and increase our focus and concentration. It makes us more compassionate, aids emotional regulation, and a strong meditation practice is also a form of discipline. Meditation is the key to so much of our self mastery, so of course it must be in the toolkit and strategies for LeaderZEN. And I don't think this is a surprise to any of us. We can't not talk about it, when we talk about the mind and mindset.

If we're looking to master our minds, we have to train them and rest them; meditation does both. If we're looking to increase focus, this is a practice of focusing on one thing and improving our concentration as we continue to encourage our wandering mind to come back to the point of focus time and again.

And yet, meditation and mindfulness have become so popular and almost overused in organisational wellness activities, that I worry the impact may get lost, especially for senior leaders. Having said that, some of the most successful senior leaders still prioritise their meditation practice, along with some of the most successful athletes.

Given its popularity, most of us will have tried it, and potentially dabbled in some kind of regular practice on and off. Those who are already further down this path of self mastery and mental fitness may already have their own regular practice, like so many other successful leaders. This will not be a 'how to meditate' chapter, but let's talk about the benefits, and strategies for leaders to embrace this key practice.

Mindfulness by definition is awareness; it's being in the present, and focusing on one thing at a time, one moment at a time.

When we rest our mind and still it, by being present and mindful, it becomes a more positive place. We're then able to hear the important stuff through the noise of the busyness. It doesn't have to be meditation either – being present is enough. Watching the sunset, becoming aware of our breathing, writing in a gratitude journal, or being in the flow of catching a wave while surfing; all are examples of being mindfully aware and in the present.

Before we can cultivate a positive mindset, we must make room in the mind and calm its busyness. If our minds are busy and full, we struggle to think straight.

For me, it's about having a toolkit to tap into when my brain becomes busy. It's taking some deep breaths each morning before I begin my day, or recentring after a tough meeting. When we still our mind, the important stuff floats to the top, rather than the noise of all the busyness we're constantly faced with.

The first few years of my meditation practice was a constant practising of focus, – a back and forth of thinking and not thinking – getting distracted and then coming back. This actually is the practice – it's how we hone our concentration. We train the brain to return to the present, each time it drifts away. The nature of our mind is to think, so thoughts will always be there. The magic happens when we start to access the space between our thoughts. Slowly this small pause between thoughts starts to get longer, and we create a space and stillness that is difficult to put into words.

I've been on a number of silent retreats where, apart from eating and sleeping, all we do is meditate. It's a constant practice of thinking in the stillness, and training our brains to focus; to be present, to be aware. It's basically hours of taming the wandering mind.

From these retreats, here are my top tips:

Top tips for practising the art of concentration

- Spend time in stillness and quiet regularly
- Become aware
- Observe your thoughts (without analysing or attaching to them)
- Notice distractions and practise concentration by bringing your focus back to the present
- Go slowly and don't expect perfection

The best practical strategies to train the brain are all really the same thing. Whether we call it mindfulness, meditation, or conscious breathing, it's the art of being in the present. It's the art of practicing concentration on one thing at a time and the art of being still and quiet. It sounds so easy, yet can be the most difficult thing to achieve in a world that prioritises busyness, doing and noise. Simply sitting still and noticing the breath or noticing five things that are going on around you is practicing being present. As with anything. the more we practise, the better we get at it, and each time we focus on the present and still the mind we're cultivating a magnificent mind.

Given what we've learned, it makes sense to look after our minds and make an effort to rest them, but how often do we spend time taking care of them?

It can be the opposite – we spend time filling our minds with social media feeds, bad news stories, rubbish TV, stress, worries about the future and regrets about the past.

Everything we put into our mind has an impact on the kind of mindset we're cultivating. This includes the people we hang out with, the gossip we engage in, the news we watch, the TV shows we consume and, of course, our social media diet.

Our relationship with technology impacts our mindset massively, so we can't not talk about it here.

Whilst technology has revolutionised the way we live and work, we are now starting to see the mental health impacts of our constant connection to devices and how this overloads our already busy brain.

Now, I don't think technology is bad; it's amazing, and it has some real life-improving uses, not just for keeping in touch with friends and family overseas, but disaster management, health apps, and more. It's an important tool for my business – but as it's also important for my health and performance, I monitor the amount of time I spend using it.

It's not so much technology that's the problem, but rather, our relationship with it. Like everything, in moderation it can be good. If we can use our devices rather than having them use us, we'll be a lot healthier and happier.

We also know that too much time on our devices is not good for stress or our focus, and it makes us feel more exhausted. Quite simply put, overuse compromises our brain and detracts from peak performance.

We used to have many pauses during our normal day. Time to rest and reset the mind. Times we waited – for the kettle to boil, the bus to arrive, the lift to the next floor, the checkout queue. Now, during those times that our minds used to be idling, resting and checking in with ourselves, we are absorbing many more thoughts, emotions and information.

Most people report that their minds feel busy, full and overloaded; some would even go as far as to say crazy, stressed, anxious or depressed. Scrolling through our devices or spending four hours a day on social media is going to make this worse, not better.

If it's the first thing we reach for when we wake up, we may have looked at the weather forecast, checked the news headlines, replied to friends' messages, watched a few cat videos, scrolled through some Instagram photos and liked a few Facebook posts, all before we've even got out of bed.

Imagine how much information we've just placed in our busy brain, before we even get up and think about the day ahead and the things we have to do – and we wonder why we can't think straight. A similar routine might play out at the end of the day, when we go to bed, and we wonder why we struggle to sleep.

According to recent findings, the average person checks their phone about 63 times a day.

Eighty-seven per cent of us do it one hour before going to bed, while 69 per cent of us check smartphones within five minutes of waking up.

When we're lost in our device, we're less present and, as a result, much more distracted; to the point where some of us can't cross the road safely anymore, such is our attachment to our device.

We live in a digitally distracted world. Technology is key to how we live our life, yet it impacts our mental health and our ability to perform. So how do we balance this?

I've removed my notifications – when I check my emails or Facebook, it's just once or twice a –day, and something I do intentionally. I've not been tricked into logging on for the tenth time that day because of a red notification badge. It also means if I pick my phone up to check the weather, I don't get distracted by a notification and find myself 30 minutes later watching videos of baby goats.

Allow your device to monitor your usage and set goals or downtime periods, so your device is actually helping you develop healthier habits around its usage. Use the data it collects to be aware of how much you're using your device and specific apps, and get an idea of what's reasonable for you.

Set times for checking messages and media – maybe in the morning and then after lunch – and resolve not to pick up your device between times. Don't keep it close at hand. Have device-free zones in the house. The dinner table and the bedroom are great starting points. Or a no-devices-after-9 pm rule might work for your family.

I'm currently trialling a rule where I don't take it to bed. It's hard when so many of us use it as an alarm, but if it's in the bedroom, it's likely to be the first thing we look at in the morning and the last thing we do before sleep. We know the LED screen interrupts our melatonin production, therefore interfering with sleep. If we wake up in the middle of the night, scrolling is the worst thing we can do if we want to get back to sleep.

Going to sleep is supposed to be a time we slow down the brain, begin to unplug and switch off. We can't do this if we're scrolling through the news and checking our emails.

This is even more important where our work device is concerned, because all that becomes much more stressful and overwhelming, if it's work emails and staff conversations on Slack invading our bedroom at night.

Yes, we all have busy lives and challenges in the real world, but that's even more reason to create the space in our brain to process and deal with this, rather than busying it further with our device habits and information overload.

It's also why I try to make a device-free day once a month. I switch off my phone and put it in a drawer, even if it's just from 8 am to 8 pm on a Sunday. It's amazing what a break our mind gets when we do this, and how much more time we find in our day to do other things.

A number of my clients this year are focusing on their relationships with social media and distractions, as part of their development. It's a bid to get more time back in their life; less noise, less overwhelm and information overload. After all, it's not just the amount of information our device exposes us to, it's also the way this information can make us feel.

One of the quickest wins for getting more focus and time is examining our relationship with social media, and devices in general. After all they are designed to distract us and, once they've got our attention, designed to make sure we waste as much time scrolling as possible.

If you're looking to reduce your information overload and the distractions of your device or social media, use some of the tips in this chapter to help.

We know a magnificent mind at its cognitive peak requires clarity, calm, space and focus, and we know that too much scrolling on our devices compromises this.

If we clear our minds of busy thoughts and cultivate clarity, we find we're closer to the state of flow that we'll explore next. When our minds are at their most focused and we are giving 100 per cent of our concentration to what we're doing, we're likely to be 'in flow' – another key component of peak performance and the ability to focus.

CREATING SPACE FOR FOCUS AND FLOW

"If you don't create and control your environment, your environment will control you." – Marshall Goldsmith

A mentally fit mind is one that can perform and has the energy needed to deliver. A focused mind is one that's clear and balanced, with awareness and a cognitive sharpness that make ideas easier to create and problems easier to solve.

If we're able to focus and have a clear, calm mind we're also in the best state to tap into flow, which has further performance and productivity benefits.

Have you ever found yourself so completely immersed in a task that the hours flew by unnoticed? Or been so absorbed in what you were doing, the doing became the goal? It's often when we're feeling most energised and accomplished that we are likely to be in the effortless state of performance known as 'flow'.

Flow is defined as an optimal state of presence and consciousness, where we feel our best and perform at our best. Fortune 500 companies, Navy Seals, and elite sports teams all teach their people how to trigger flow to create cutting-edge performances.

When we're in flow it's likely we'll feel full of energy, our productivity will increase, we'll be more creative and innovative, and feel more confident and happier.

Flow researcher and author Steven Kotler reports flow can increase creativity by 400 per cent and learning uptake by 240 to 500 per cent.

In a 10-year McKinsey study, top executives reported being five times more productive when in flow. That means if we spent Monday in flow, we could literally take the rest of the week off and still have done more than most.

Most of us spend less than five per cent of our work life in flow. If that number could be nudged up closer to 20 per cent, according to the same McKinsey study, overall workplace productivity would almost double. That's a significant shift on the dial where performance is concerned.

Research by flow guru Mihaly Csikszentmihalyi tells us that to create flow, an activity must stretch our potential enough to have an even balance between how challenging the activity feels for us, and our level of skill to complete the activity. This is known as the 'challenge to skill ratio'.

Commonly described as being in the zone, we are totally absorbed in the task, oblivious to everything going on around us, and merging at one with the activity. Flow is often attributed to athletes and artists but is available to us all.

It describes those moments of focus when we're using our skills, being stretched enough to feel challenged and accomplished; creating something with meaning and totally absorbed in that. It's more challenging than tasks that are too easy or boring, but not so much that we're out of our depth or worried we can't do it. It's also when we're in control and know we're capable too.

Csikszentmihalyi's Eight Characteristics of Flow:

- Complete concentration on the task
- Clarity of goals and reward in mind and immediate feedback

- Transformation of time
- The experience is intrinsically rewarding
- Effortlessness
- There is a balance between challenge and skills
- Actions and awareness are merged, losing self-conscious rumination
- There is a feeling of control over the task

Those in flow describe being in a flow state as timeless; they say they feel content, serene, focused, completely involved and forget all else. They experience a connection to something bigger, and inner clarity.

We only have a finite amount of attention and focus, so if we're spreading it across many things, it makes sense that we're not going to produce quality from that period of time. It's like being in a meeting and thinking about what's for dinner, reading the notes from the last meeting, and checking our emails, as people talk around us. However, if we focus all of our energy or attention on one thing, we can imagine how the quality would improve.

When we're focusing on one thing at a time and absorbed in that with all our attention and effort, of course it's going to be a better-quality output.

Tips to create flow

- Practise mindfulness – a present mind is a focused one
- Do things that use your skills/strengths
- Develop healthy habits (sleep, eat, move)
- Regulate your emotional response
- Seek a healthy level of challenge and stretch
- Take regular breaks
- Avoid distractions

The reason we want to be in flow is because that is when we are at our best, most focused, and productive, therefore giving 100 per cent to what we're doing. It's also when we're able to access deep work.

'Deep work' is a phrase coined by Cal Newport, a *professor* at Georgetown University, and a New York Times bestselling author.

Newport describes deep work as: "Professional activities performed in a state of distraction-free concentration that push your cognitive capabilities to their limit. These efforts create new value, improve your skill and are hard to replicate."

Like flow, it is the ability to focus without distraction on a cognitively demanding task. A skill that allows us to quickly master complicated information and produce better results in less time.

It's carving out the thinking space to come up with our best ideas.

According to Newport, deep work makes us better at what we do, but our environment and equipment are not always enablers. Most of us have lost the art of going deep or we don't allow ourselves the space.

We have to be intentional about getting into this state, otherwise we run the risk of busying our way through our to-do list, only ever being in a 'shallow work' mode.

It's why I schedule retreats for myself; I go away to plan my year ahead. I go away to write. It's just me in a rural Airbnb somewhere with no distractions. I put my phone away, turn my notifications off and don't check emails. This allows me the space to think, to create and to do deep work.

It's also why I was never a fan of the open plan office (that and being an introvert). I struggled to go into a state of deep work and fully focus with so many distractions around me.

It turns out that Managed Isolation Quarantine is a distraction free environment for deep work. In fact, that is where I wrote my previous book, in an attempt at using my time productively whilst in quarantine after visiting my UK-based family during the Covid-19 pandemic. There were no distractions; I wasn't allowed out to do anything other than write. Having said that though, it was missing some of my usual environmental requirements for creativity like fresh air and sunshine.

But we don't have to go on a retreat to do deep work, or even leave the office. It's about creating an environment for us to focus. When I'm doing deep work my phone is always on silent, I let my voicemail pick up calls and return them later.

But don't just take my advice. Newport himself advises we focus on four elements to achieve deep work: location, duration, structure and requirements.

So, for example; working at home with the office door closed or putting your mobile in your bag on silent.

Or setting a duration to intentionally allow for a focus on deep work and adding the structure that makes it happen, for example; putting the phone away and the computer on 'do not disturb' until you've written 10,000 words.

And lastly, the final touches – the things required to make this a success. It might be having water nearby, and the laptop charger plugged in, or putting on your favourite focus-music on your headphones.

Whether it's flow or deep work, we're talking about creating space to do our best work; to allow for focus and to improve productivity. It can feel counter-intuitive to diary thinking time, or space. In a society that has prioritised busy and doing, taking time to think and create space (especially on company time) can feel indulgent.

In Zen practices we talk a lot about space: observing the space of the present moment, creating space in our minds, and of course, there's the physical space all around us.

For leaders, gaining space has so many benefits. Space in our schedule is a gift we don't always afford ourselves, and yet is critical for strategic thinking, creativity, and getting to all that big stuff we've put on the back burner. It's in this space where flow is more likely to occur and where we add the most value and impact. Also, of course, there are the self-care and sustainability practices we can do when we have the space, and so often, a lack of space and time is our reason for not getting to the foundational performance rituals that keep us at our best.

And lastly, there's the physical space we have around us; how ordered and simple that is (or not) and the impact this has on our mental load and sense of overwhelm.

On the subject of simplifying, let's talk briefly about this aspect of Zen, because it helps lessen the load and create space. An example that springs to mind is the simplicity of dress for monks and nuns and the impact of a simple uniform that became popular through The Minimalists and was adopted by some top executives. For monks and nuns, it's a symbol of simplicity and austerity, it's not about having nothing. The simple monastic lifestyle is about having what you need and not needing more. It's not that you own nothing but that you only have what you need. 'Letting go' is a popular Zen concept; it opens the mind and prepares the ground for self mastery and deeper spiritual development. Now, not all of that sounds like it's transferable into leadership, yet letting go and simplifying can do wonders for our overloaded brains. Some top CEOs talk about a limited amount of clothes they use as a uniform for work (much easier if you're male) and the reason behind this is to reduce the mental load. It's one less decision to have to make that day.

Clearing out our wardrobe might sound more Marie Kondo than LeaderZEN, but it's a valuable concept that we can apply to our work, our overloaded schedules, and our brains. We tend to think that the more we have, the better life will be, and yet simplicity is probably the most underrated approach to an abundant life. The less we have, the less there is to worry about. The fewer decisions we must make, the more space we free up in our brain. In the same way, the more stimulation we have mentally, the more we then need to feel stimulated. Simplicity is often the shortcut to creating more space both externally and internally.

It is common in Zen traditions to make space for reflection and contemplation. We spend a lot of time thinking. This doesn't always translate well to the leadership space where 'doing' has always been more heavily weighted. Yes, I agree that action is paramount to our success, but it shouldn't be the only mode we operate in across a day or a week. We've not always given priority to space, thinking time, contemplation or reflection. We falsely see the most impact in action and doing; productivity in tangible jobs we can tick off a list. Yet from a value and impact perspective, the thinking and reflection time can be the most important thing we do all week.

Even when we do make the time, we're not quite sure what to do with it, or feel guilty for not doing something more action orientated that we can tick off a list and call productivity.

Reflection is how we learn, and it also increases our performance. It's a short cut to making us more self-aware too. A 2014 study done at HEC Paris, Harvard Business School, and the University of North Carolina showed a 23 per cent better performance in groups that reflected after a learning experience, compared to those that did not.

When it comes to accelerating performance, there's a paradox: if we want to have greater impact, faster, we have to slow down enough to reflect on what we've done and what we're going to do.

I've always loved learning from other cultures, and ancient wisdom in particular. We tend to see these things come back into fashion and pitched to our Western world as the new solution, and yet they are never really that new. Yoga was ancient wisdom well before lululemon found it. Monks were meditating well before mindfulness become fashionable, and Maori ancestors were well versed in our connection to the land and living in harmony with the natural world before climate change was on the agenda.

In particular though, I've always marvelled at how ancient cultures all over the world have valued the concept of space and time to think. Whether it's monks in caves, pilgrimages, or aboriginal walkabouts, there are many examples of people prioritising space and solitude – getting away from it all and just being. It's also a practice that cultivates deep connection to something bigger, and, in many ancient cultures, is a practice considered to make us wiser.

I couldn't agree more and it's the foundational practice that has enabled me to innovate, problem solve, get perspective, and gain greater clarity, which is why I'm a passionate advocate.

However, in our busy modern lives we've deprioritised space and quiet in favour of busyness, noise and doing. We live in a world of information overload, fast living and full schedules where we think we can get more done, yet the quality and value of what we're doing has been suffering for years. I believe the answer lies in cultivating this space and quiet. As Ram Dass said, "the quieter you become, the more you can hear."

This thinking space is so crucial. It's where we innovate, it's how we think strategically, it's how we process our thoughts and calm our minds, and it's how we focus and gain clarity to make decisions and solve problems. Not to mention the impact it has on overwhelm, stress and our emotional regulation.

The practice of being by ourselves and getting some quiet space helps improve our focus and concentration, and tap into a different part of the brain. Yet it's a practice we've become uncomfortable doing and have undervalued for too long. It's not easy to sit with our own thoughts these days, but it's possibly the most impactful thing we can do.

I don't mean we need to find a cave to meditate in. It's making the most of our moments; the purposeful pauses throughout our day. Detaching from our devices for a few hours. Spending some time in nature. Being by ourselves and not listening to, watching, or reading anything. Being present in our surroundings. Journaling. Going for a walk or a swim.

I believe it's where we create the most value and impact, both in life and in work, when we give the brain space to think. It's where our best ideas come from and where we gain clarity and focus. Yes, we need implementation, but if we don't leave space for thinking there's nothing great to implement.

I often take myself off to the beach for the day, go kayaking, or go for a bush walk. To most people it probably looks like a day off. I'm pretty sure my wife doesn't think I'm working. However, this is a key part of my job and central to my success. This is my thinking space. It's where I create, have ideas or mull over problems. What might look in the diary like a day off can result in my biggest breakthroughs or my next bestseller. Now, my brain can't achieve what it does at these times if I'm in the office checking emails. It requires the space to tap into its most innovative capacity and it's from here these thoughts flow.

I'd encourage you to seek the difference between quality and quantity – consider how you add impact and value above hours worked and busy distractions. Where can you carve out time and space in your schedule to think?

The fact that we're too busy to pause is the precise reason we need it so badly. Whilst writing my last book, *Burnout to Brilliance,* I discovered it's often our pursuit of peak performance and the 'more is always better' mantra that are in fact leading us to burnout. The pursuit of brilliance leads us to burnout –ironic, right? But it doesn't have to be this way.

Our high-achiever drive keeps us pushing, and often struggles when we take time to just be, because we're not getting the high of doing, or the satisfaction of results, when we're taking time out. We don't get the instant gratification of ticking off the to-do list and the positive impacts come much further down the track (less stress, better emotional regulation, increased focus, concentration, innovation, resilience, clarity and energy).

For many of us, our self-worth and value have been built on how much we achieve and how useful we can be to others. We get uncomfortable if we're not contributing or being useful. It's why it's so easy to throw ourselves into constant busyness – it also distracts us from any problems we have and can wind up like an addictive drug for our brains.

If you've ever had time off between jobs, or recovery time from burnout, you may have noticed you were tempted to fill it with baking, learning a new language, training to run a marathon, or major house renovations. I was no different, choosing to travel the world and write my first book during my burnout recovery. Fortunately for me, part of that journey was living in ashrams and going on silent retreats which forced me to slow down, to be still, and to master the art of being, not doing. It's through this experience I have gained the insight into the value of doing nothing.

Our devices have also trained our minds to be constantly absorbing. We are always looking for information or entertainment to fill a void. Every time we get a second to ourselves, we pick up our phones and seek to fill in the time or distract ourselves from the stillness. Our brains are no longer conditioned to reflect; to be in the present; to idle or to rest. We get impatient, thanks to that instant gratification muscle that continues to flex and take us away from this critical skill.

Often the stillness gives rise to the best ideas, the energy to deliver, and the sustainability to be our best, without burning out in the process. Our brains can't think or create when they're in busy or doing mode. Tapping into the creative part of the brain and thinking is a different art; one that requires space. Some of the most impactful things that have happened to my business have been thanks to the ideas I've had when I was not in the office working.

Next time you have a day off, don't schedule anything. Try sitting for an hour (or walking) without distractions and be in the moment. Practise the art of reflection or encourage some stillness into your day. It might seem uncomfortable at first, for all the reasons we've discussed, and yet it could be your secret weapon in achieving leadership excellence.

Set a reflection meeting with yourself to reoccur in your calendar. My "self-meetings" are probably the most important ones I have for my business, whether it's planning, creating or reflecting.

If you're struggling for space, leverage the power of the pause. This is a chance to reset and clear the mind. Whether it's a walk around the block or getting up early to enjoy some peace and solitude over a cup of tea, find a way to carve out mini moments to reset your brain, find space, and reap the rewards.

After writing six books, I've experimented with a number of techniques and have found a focused retreat the quickest and most effective way of getting the words on a page. (Albeit a very rough first draft!) People have asked me, "How do you know you'll be creative on that week though, and be able to write?"

The answer is I don't. But I do know how to set my environment up to make that more likely to happen. For me, that's no social media or calls. No emails or internet. It's a change of scenery that's not my own house or office, so nothing else needs doing other than writing. I have all the supplies I need, and I shut myself away, alone in a beautiful cottage by the beach if possible, and often rural.

On the days when I don't feel the creative muse, I go for a walk, or make some food, or sit outside in the sun, to mix things up and flick the creative switch on. The most important thing for me is creating the space and not having the distractions. Without doing that I know I'm much less creative.

Interruptions are a barrier to focus and flow, and indeed our productivity, which is why space away from them is so important. 'Interruption Science' is the study of the effect of disruptions on job performance, especially for those working in an office environment. According to a University of California, Irvine (UCI) study, regaining our initial momentum following an interruption can take, on average, upwards of 20 minutes. It makes it more difficult to get anything done, and actually means we are taking longer to get tasks completed by not giving them our full attention and trying to multitask.

An experiment conducted at the University of London found that we lose as many as 10 IQ points when we allow our work to be interrupted. That's the equivalent to missing a whole night's sleep, and more than double the four-point fall seen after smoking marijuana. Even short interruptions are thought to have a negative impact, for example, silencing the phone, or just checking the screen to see who's calling. That's even when we decide not to answer because we don't want to be distracted. A study by Michigan State University, in which 300 people performed a sequence-based procedure on a computer, found that interruptions of about three seconds doubled the error rate.

Author Pico Iyer talks of interruption science in his book *The Art of Stillness*. He says: "It takes 25 minutes to recover from things like a phone call, yet such interruptions come every 11 minutes, so we never really catch up with ourselves."

When we're creating space to increase our focus, concentration, and awareness, we're also preparing it for calm. Why is this important and how can we use it to make ourselves better leaders?

EQUANIMITY: CALM IS CONTAGIOUS

"You are the sky. Everything else – it's just the weather."
– Pema Chödrön

The person in room with the most control is generally the one with the lowest heart rate. When you're in control of yourself you don't need to control others.

I was chatting to Dr Ashley Bloomfield at a recent speaker event at our speaking agency. We were talking about the importance of calm and how it promotes trust. I said to him, "During those pandemic briefings on TV it didn't really matter what you were saying; we all believed you and felt like you had it covered. You delivered it with such calmness you appeared to be in control and competent." I meant it as a compliment of course but may have had a wine beforehand.

It's true though – when a leader is flustered or angry, we feel uneasy, and it seeps into the team. Yet when they present calmly, we trust they have things in hand.

This has rung true for me during some of the toughest times in my leadership journey. For example, when a staff member had died by suicide, having to drop everything to go to a meeting room where their team and manager had gathered. Not only to speak to them, but also to arrange the logistics of support and communication across the business, and bring the rest of the staff together to announce the news and manage the subsequent aftermath. What many have said to me during times like that has been; "You were so calm." Often our calm can be contagious; it puts others at ease when we enter a room, before we've even said a word.

Calm also allows us to operate from a place of grounded clarity. Our brains change when in fight or flight mode, and when we're stressed or worried, we don't perform as well. We can't, because our bodies decide to focus on the physiological stuff that'll keep us alive, not how well we can articulate the brief.

It's something I learned in the early days of my speaking career: to manage public speaking nerves. Taking a few breaths or doing a meditation on the way to the venue meant I was far less likely to forget my lines, and I always performed better.

The skill of equanimity is one of remaining calm, even-tempered and composed, regardless of what's happening around us. It's the cool head in the heat of the moment and helps us cultivate patience.

I like to think of it like the ocean. Each day, depending on the weather, the surface can be different; sometimes the waves are high and it's quite rough. It's impacted by whatever the weather is doing, and yet below the surface the water is always still, quiet and calm. We get a sense of this when diving or snorkelling.

It's a core aspect of Zen traditions, whether that's martial arts or Buddhist meditation. Many hours of meditation are spent understanding and experiencing that uncomfortable things can happen, and yet inside we can remain equanimous. It's often not what happens to us, but our reaction to it.

"Are you saying I can't get angry as a leader?" No – I don't mean not experiencing any of the raft of normal human emotions, including anger. It's about what we do with them and how we allow them to affect our state, or not. Equanimity is not about suppressing emotions, but remaining calm and grounded whilst the emotion passes through us. This means we might still experience anger, but when we do, we'll be able to respond rather than react, and that response will come from a place of equanimity, meaning it'll be a much more positive one. It'll also mean we won't experience any of the physical and mental side effects that often come when our emotions get the better of us.

What makes the mind calm is often the same stuff that increases our awareness and cognitive function. It's the things we've talked about in self mastery and how we respond to change. When we have mastered our mind and cleared it of its clutter, it is infinitely more calm.

There are other things we can do to change our state and bring calm to our lives, and this depends on personal preference. For some it's a walk on the beach or time in nature; others prefer music to change their state and there are plenty of calming playlists to pick from. Still others need solitude and space to ground in, and for some it's a run, surf or swim – something more active. We also have calming associations; maybe a type of smell (lavender, for example, if a parent used it on your pillow when you were young). Or maybe it's your favourite candle or incense, a certain comfortable jumper, or a cushion that gives you that feeling that all is well. Even just stopping and taking three deep breaths will help increase our calm.

How many of us have statues of Buddha in our garden? It is said in Buddhism that just seeing an image of Buddha is calming, which is possibly why we have them in spas and in our gardens.

Where equanimity is concerned though, it's cultivating this calm and working on our mind, so we remain in this state regardless of physical objects and circumstances.

You can probably see now how much of this is focused on the mind. It's the centre of most Zen studies too. We've looked at mental fitness and a resilient mind. We've looked at the benefits of improved cognitive function through a clear, focused mind as well as the role space must play in increasing our innovation and calm. Another role the mind plays is curiosity and our ability to learn – also important for leadership development.

BEGINNER'S MIND: CONSTANT LEARNER

"You are allowed to be both a masterpiece and a work in progress simultaneously." – Sophia Bush

Do you speak to give knowledge or listen to gain it? There's a place for both and as a leader, ensuring there's a balance of both is crucial.

In the past, knowledge has been power and there's been a pressure for leaders to know all the answers, or to be the ones telling others what they think or how something should be done. This means it gets done your way but not necessarily the best way.

Growth and development, an area I've worked in for years, is a passion I've always had. I believe we can be both improving and learning as well as being amazing and brilliant – all at once. Buddhists speak of the beginner's mind – approaching everything with a curiosity that we're here to learn, even if we've done it before, because the reality is we're always learning; there's always growth. We're always a beginner even when we're an expert.

Ako is a traditional Māori practice that means both "to learn" and "to teach" and I think that sums it up perfectly.

Even as teachers we're always learning. I love this idea of continuous learning; that we never know it all and that life itself is a constant navigation of learning; often teaching others at the same time as we're learning ourselves.

They say the best way to learn something is to teach it and I've certainly found that when embarking on book projects. Teaching this stuff to others helps me immerse myself in it, in a way that furthers my own learning and understanding. We so often learn by teaching and yet at the same time are also still learning whilst we teach.

We put so much pressure on ourselves to know all the answers, or be the expert, that it can be uncomfortable to sit in this place of learning; of not knowing. But it's this open and curious mind that keeps us developing and growing and helps us achieve our potential.

It's this theory of improving ourselves rather than trying to prove ourselves – that we're learning and growing, not trying to validate or prove we're good enough.

No matter how much experience or how many awards or titles we have, we're still learning. It's retaining this curiosity, and the awareness that we never know it all, that keeps us agile and open to things we may otherwise miss.

In leadership, it has long been the custom to give weight to academic qualifications, letters after our name, or our titles and status. Yet lived experience can be where our best leadership moments come from.

We can learn a lot of theory and we do (there are hundreds of leadership courses you can take). Yet the experience we have of what we learn is what helps us understand and bring to life the real lesson.

To know something intellectually is different to knowing it on an experiential level.

"To accept some idea of truth without experiencing it is like a painting of a cake on paper which you cannot eat." – Suzuki Roshi

I wanted to learn to surf for many years before I eventually did. I'd study YouTube clips and watch others but as the famous saying goes; you can't learn to surf without getting wet. It was only by getting in the water that I really learned.

I believe there are three levels of knowing; intellectual knowing is the first. I might look out to the ocean. The second is checking for understanding; I might ask others who've been out in it what it was like. The third of course is the experience and the doing, and this is the only point at which I can truly know what it's like to surf. It's a little bit like gardeners who subscribe to the magazines and yet have a garden full of weeds.

"Knowing without doing is the same as not knowing" is one of my favourite Buddhist proverbs. In the West we have a thirst for knowledge and to know so many things. Yet, if we do nothing with it and don't experience what we've learned, we may as well not have learnt it. It's about bringing the lesson to life through action and experience; this is how we truly know.

Once we understand our levels of knowing, we are far more likely to reap rewards from our knowledge, and be motivated to draw on the experience of others. This is particularly important when promoting diversity of thought. Collaboration and lived experiences ensure inclusion and strengthen diversity.

I'm the first to admit, regardless of what I'm speaking about, that I'm not the only expert in the room. The richness of the conversations and the resulting ideas and new thoughts I then have from those events can prove invaluable.

Last year I got into a habit of re-reading books I've already read. I'd never thought of it until someone suggested it to me. My friend made a valid point. We don't retain most of the information when we read something the first time, and we're a different person now than we were five years ago when we read it, so we'll probably get a different value from it. There might be things we didn't understand, or forgot completely, or just make more sense now. It's a way of revisiting ideas and seeing how they apply now. I've really enjoyed re-reading some of the books that changed my life. If you're keen to find out what they are, there's a recommended reading list on my website.

Remaining curious means that we're more likely to collaborate and accept we're not the only expert in the room. My first meditation teacher, Kelsang Demo, a nun, was in her seventies when she passed, but right up to that point would camp in the bush, go on multi-day hikes, and had learned to livestream her dharma talks and record audio to create distance learning options.

It takes a lot of courage to admit to not knowing, or to seek help and support. It's a courageous act for a leader to embrace this beginner's mind and commit to being a constant learner. It also requires keeping the ego in check, which is an aspect of Zen we've yet to cover.

This is a deep topic and one I don't feel qualified to teach, and yet there are key understandings that come from the concept of ego and emptiness that I think are applicable here. Let's touch lightly on ego and the way it relates to LeaderZEN.

Buddhism teaches that the cause of our suffering is clinging to what we believe to be our "self" or "ego". When we feel unsafe or uncertain, our habitual defences arise, causing us to cling even more defensively to our ego.

Ego is often linked to the act of grasping and attachment – something we desperately want for ourselves that we cling on to tightly. There's a wonderful Buddhist saying that I often use myself when I can feel this happening: "Hold on tight with an open palm". This can be especially useful with opinions, or ways in which we think things should happen, according to our wishes. We can have an opinion, or a preference, and we can hold that tightly, but we must also be flexible and open enough for that to change.

Hence the open palm.

Ego can also make us want to appear superior to others in order to feel good about ourselves. When we're busy finding fault in others, it's often wise to ask how much of this is used to distract from our own insecurities. It's hard to collaborate or listen when ego is at play, or to admit that you might not be the only expert in the room.

We can tell that ego is at play when we fear what people will say, when we compare to others, want to prove ourselves, or pretend we know everything. It also impacts our response if we believe we've been wronged or something that "belongs" to us is threatened.

For example, a $1,000 watch breaks just after you bought it and you're devastated because it's *your* watch. The same watch that breaks at exactly the same time on somebody else's wrist, or in the shop before you buy it, doesn't hurt you half as much because it's not yours. When we feel attachment and ownership to this sense of "I" or "mine" we can become more defensive and indignant.

In psychology, ego refers to the psychological construct that is our identity. We need our egos to navigate the world, to regulate our instincts, to exercise our executive function, and to mediate the conflicting demands of self and other. So it's less about dissolving our ego and more about our relationship with it.

This can translate into leadership in how we show up in meetings, handle conflict, relate to our team and peers, and in managing up. Ego can also be attached to our status and role title, especially as we become more senior. When ego becomes a cause for concern, we'll notice things like a belief: "This is the way I am so things should be as *I* believe they should be". If something differs from our expectations, we get angry. Selfishness can also emerge at this point.

Ego is often the person we change into when important people are watching, or donating to the school only if our name is published in the magazine so everyone knows it was us. Or when we're queuing our fabulous story in response to a friend who's not even finished theirs – that we've only been half listening to.

Ego is a huge barrier to self mastery and such an easy trap to fall into. Not to be confused with confidence, managing our ego takes courage. Selfless leaders are courageous and when they understand their power, they no longer need to prove themselves or have the last word. The dissolution of ego is one of the hardest and most self-assured things we can do, yet it comes with humility, not arrogance.

There's a certain humility that offsets the ego. It's not about lack of confidence, but self-esteem in who we are and what we bring, without the arrogance of thinking we know everything. This humility allows us to learn and to be open.

The point is, when you're satisfied with who you are and have the self-efficacy to stand in your power, you don't need to prove yourself or impress others and the ego will stop puffing itself up.

My take on this has always been that your sweet spot is the awareness to know what you're good at, and the humility not to be an ass about it. Ego desires respect but humility inspires it.

Once we are aware of the ego and when it is at play, the best advice is to try detaching from it. It's almost like we are watching a movie. We observe thoughts and feelings without trying to analyse or attach to them. This opens up space between the stimulus (our thought) and the response, which allows us to respond rather than react.

There's a famous Buddhist saying regarding enlightenment, which is said to be the highest attainment for a Zen master and includes the dissolution of the ego: "Before enlightenment chop wood and carry water. After enlightenment chop wood and carry water." No matter who you are or what your superiority we're all the same, and undertaking menial tasks, whether you're a novice monk or a Zen master, helps us keep that in mind. The same can be true for leaders.

HABITS FOR MASTERY

"We are what we repeatedly do. Excellence, then, is not an act, but a habit." —Aristotle

What if it all seems too much? It's not practical to expect leaders to also be monks; there's a middle way, and this book is about giving you the information so you can decide what resonates and what you'd like to do with it. My advice is the same as my teacher and nun Kelsang Gen Demo gave me. "Take the bits that resonate for you and just leave the rest to one side".

Having spent time living in ashrams, monastic communities and with monks and nuns, the thing I've always admired is the discipline. The discipline to get up at 4 am, stick to a strict schedule, and abstain from so many things by undertaking precepts such as: celibacy, not eating after noon, refraining from alcohol or drugs, and not partaking in any luxuries or sensual pleasures, etc. The precepts are like a moral code linked back to the Buddhist eight-fold path that consists of: right view, right aspiration, right speech, right conduct, right livelihood, right effort, right mindfulness and right concentration. It takes tremendous discipline.

When we talk about habits, discipline is the essential ingredient. I'm not suggesting leaders would be more effective if they took the precepts, although some might be useful to practise in moderation! It's the discipline that precepts or any kind of moderation require that we can translate into our leadership practice for impact.

After all, high performance comes from setting good habits. This is certainly what I've seen work for me, and the recurring theme I've observed amongst high-performing leaders I've worked with.

How they look after themselves and build resilience is key, and impacts their mindset, which we know is often the difference between success and failure. The key to getting those bits right, though, often is within the habits they form.

It sounds simple, but it's not. Otherwise, we'd all go to the gym, eat salad and wake up at 6 am.

A habit is a repeated behaviour that becomes automatic. The trouble is we tend to find it easier to keep the bad habits and harder to form good ones, which often require more effort and offer less immediate reward.

How can we build positive habits and break bad ones? The best advice I've heard on this topic comes from James Clear, in his book *Atomic Habits*. Clear believes both success and failure are preceded by habits, and we can be the creator of our habits, not the victim. What's on our desk or how we set up our home can influence our behaviours and habits – often, he says, our environment is the architect of our habits.

What I like about focusing on our habits is it puts us in control; it's something we can influence. Whilst we tend to think success is down to talent, and some people are high performers just because of talent, there's much more to it. Talent gets us so far, but great habits make the difference. This is true when we hear the stories of top athletes. They may have talent to start with, but so do others who've not made it in their field. The difference most of them talk about is the hard work and effort they put in, the discipline to train, the structure and routines they have, and habits they've mastered.

It's about forming good habits and repeating them consistently, whether that's your gym routine and training; or organising your diary, team one-to-ones, taking a lunch break and managing your inbox.

Let's look at breaking bad habits first, though. Reducing exposure and temptation is key. If you want to save money, unsubscribe from those marketing emails that tempt you with specials. Want to stop eating chocolate at night whilst watching TV? Don't buy it or have it in the house. If we have to get in the car and go to the shops for it, we're less likely to do it – making the bad habit harder helps break it.

Is your environment conducive to forming good habits or bad ones? Which are easier for you, and how can you make the bad ones harder to do and the good ones easier? I don't usually have biscuits in the house; it's an easy way to break my bad habit of demolishing a whole packet at once. Similarly, having my gym kit ready to go in the morning means I'm more likely to go to the gym – I've made it easier.

It's the law of least effort, according to Clear. If we make bad habits harder and good habits easier, we'll see a shift. We also need to want to do the habit (enjoy it), and have an environment that's conducive and a plan to make it happen.

The law of least effort is why it's easy to binge-watch Netflix. The environment is created in a way that means it's easier to let it keep auto playing the next episode than to pick up the device and press stop. It's why we intend to watch one episode and instead watch the whole season and stay up three hours later than planned!

So how can we form good habits and make them easier to adopt? Simply by doing that: make them easy and link them to a reward, so we enjoy doing them.

I love the sauna, but the gym takes a bit more motivation. They are based in the same building, so leaving my gym kit ready to go in the car makes it easy for me to go (or at least gives me fewer excuses not to), and then I reward myself afterwards with a sauna. I know I only get the sauna if I go to the gym, and once I'm in the building for one, the other becomes much easier to stick to.

There is another great hack from James Clear when it comes to forming good habits: habit stacking. This is adding a new habit we want to form on to an existing habit, so we're more likely to do it.

For example, I mean to take my supplements, but I often forget. Leaving them by the kettle helps remind me and makes this habit easy, because I've stacked it with another habit I know I'll do every morning – make my cup of tea.

Similarly, my meditation habit is something I do each morning at the same time my partner is walking the dog. It means the house is quiet, and it's part of my morning routine.

When we think of habits, it can become a drain – "I must do this". Reframing the thought into "the kind of person I want to become" gives it more meaning and also motivates us.

I want to be a calm, clear-headed, focused leader; that's why I meditate each morning. That's different to thinking of it as another thing on my to-do list I've got to get around to doing today. It connects with my "why" and the benefit I'm getting from this. It links my results to my beliefs. There's also the added reward-hit on my meditation app, which gives me a gold star each time I don't miss a day, because, let's face it, the reward of a calm, clear mind takes much more than one session to realise.

So, what habits do you want to form, and what's your plan of action? Having the goal is one thing, but James Clear will tell you that the habit is the system behind making that goal a reality.

Our fitness or weight-loss goals only happen because of healthy habits. Our revenue goals are realised because of our sales strategy. It's less about what we're aiming for and more about what we're going to do to get there – then the result takes care of itself.

This enables us to have a plan and develop good habits. I like the analogy Clear uses of running a race; we tend to focus on the finish line and how we ready ourselves for the result we want to see.

Clear looks at it more like being ready for the start line. If we're ready at the start line, the finish (goal) will take care of itself and eventuate by virtue of our preparation and plan (habits).

It can often seem like there's too much to do on this leadership development journey, or indeed any personal development. "There's too much to learn and I want to do it all". That brings me to the final Buddhist concept I want to talk about; one that is useful when thinking about habits and mastery; "the middle path".

The middle path, or middle way as it's sometimes known, is all about moderation and finding the middle ground.

The middle path generally refers to the avoidance of two extremes. The Buddha himself started life as a prince and renounced his luxury lifestyle, to embrace the other extreme as an ascetic practicing severe austerity.

Eventually he landed between those two extremes, ultimately realising that both indulgence and deprivation were equally useless, even detrimental, to his goal of achieving awakening.

I like to think of this and apply it to my work as moderation, finding the middle ground between excess and scarcity. I use this with perfectionists to allow for their overestimated goals and expectations. With failure at the other end, we can find a middle ground that's realistic and excellent, between failure and perfection.

It's great to use this in health goals and routines too. I might not want to run a marathon, but I don't want to be a couch potato either. I don't want to be overweight but nor do I want to be starving. Even where stress is concerned, we have the middle way of eustress; positive motivational stress which sits between boredom and burnout.

I think this can also be a useful strategy in negotiations and team collaborations. When dealing with opposing views, asking the question "What's the middle path here?" can be one of the most useful conversations to reach a consensus.

So, what's your middle path, and what will you now do with what you know?

CONCLUSION

As we come to the end of our journey together it seems timely to look back at some key points and the elements of LeaderZEN as we wrap up.

Our foundation of success is how we first lead ourselves. This is knowing ourselves and then ensuring we have the sustainability and stamina to deliver on what we're capable of. Self mastery is a process of awareness and acceptance of our strengths, weaknesses, and who we are. This not only articulates our leadership brand but also helps us lead more authentically.

We've looked at the roles of compassion and kindness, two fundamental Zen principles, and how they apply to our leadership style and can add competitive advantage. We've also looked at the empathy that comes from that and the role of emotional intelligence.

Self mastery takes discipline and can be built by development, learning, reflection practices. and gathering feedback.

Mastering the art of acceptance and impermanence are central principles of Buddhism and Zen traditions that help us navigate change and lead others through uncertain times. This is why mental fitness is so important and helps to build a magnificent mind. When we perform at our peak cognitively, everything becomes easier. We're also much more able to remain equanimous, and respond rather than react, when we are in control of our mind and have a positive mindset.

Calm is contagious, and the person in the room with the lowest heart rate is generally the one in control. Staying calm amid the chaos is a fundamental attribute of a great leader.

This involves managing distractions to improve focus and concentration, as well as cutting through the noise and busyness to focus on the high value, impact work. When we limit distractions and create space to focus, we also create the conditions for a flow state, enhancing our innovation, performance and productivity.

Creating space, not just in our minds but also in our schedules, enables all of this to happen. It promotes self mastery, improves innovation, cultivates focus and allows time. It's one of the best things we can do for our mind, yet it's a luxury we don't often allow ourselves.

A Zen leader has the curiosity to continue to learn, listen and ask. This concept transcends ego and helps us embrace a beginner's mind. It helps us collaborate, be more inclusive, and of course learn, but depends on our courage to be vulnerable and admit to not being the only expert in the room.

Leadership can be tough; keep an eye on your energy levels. When we know where we're at, we know what we need. Know when your inner fuel light is on and it's time for a recharge. This will ensure you're sustainable and can build resilience for the journey ahead.

What's the best kind of environment for you and how do you set that up, so you're set up for success? Do you have a morning routine? What's your plan A and plan B to make that happen regardless of what detours life takes?

As a result of self mastery you'll be infinitely wiser. As a result of equanimity, you'll be infinitely calmer and as a result of creating space, you'll be more innovative and focused. All of this means you'll also be performing at the next level. Your cognitive function will be sharp; you'll have strong awareness and mental fitness. Your teams will be more engaged and productive when you lead like you live, and together, you'll be able to lead through this landscape of change.

It's been my pleasure to share with you the wisdom I have such a passion for, and that I know from experience makes a difference.

Whilst we often aspire to ancient traditions and gurus to find answers, much of the wisdom that comes from Buddhism and other Zen traditions is that the guru is within us. We are our own guru and everything we need is already inside. If we invest in self mastery, we become our own guru and find the answers within.

PRACTICAL TIPS FOR ZEN LEADERS

- Set up meetings with yourself
- Embrace the power of the pause in your day
- Create your rituals for sustainability
- Embark on a suitable morning routine
- Create an environment for flow
- Reduce noise and distractions
- Develop a reflection habit
- Leverage kindness and empathy
- Lead like you live
- Know yourself – practise awareness building, know your values, and get feedback
- Meditate, or use some other mindfulness practice that grounds you and helps you stay present
- Practise some calming techniques to master the skill of equanimity
- Be curious, and comfortable not knowing it all; have a beginner's mind and be a constant learner
- Listen before you speak
- Focus on the high value work, not the noise and busyness (quality over quantity)
- Be disciplined with your boundaries

- Make sure your actions align with your priorities
- Create space and diary time for deep thinking

My love of these traditions and how we can learn from them has inspired much of my work to date. We can all go on leadership courses and learn technical skills to further our career, but it is this self mastery and inner work that really sets us apart. Awareness, wisdom, discipline and equanimity will always give us the edge. It's why Buddhism (and other traditions) refer to the highest mastery as enlightenment; to have transcended the ordinary. Not that I'm suggesting that's what will happen here and nor does it need to.

LeaderZEN is not about becoming more monk like, but rather, weaving the ancient Eastern wisdom into our modern leadership development in a way that makes us more mentally fit, productive, adaptable, calm, focused, authentic, and gives us the ability to perform at our peak and be great leaders.

If this has resonated with you, find out more about the in-house LeaderZEN training programme for you and your leadership team.

"Smile, breathe and go slowly" – Thich Nhat Hanh

RESOURCES

Jess runs leadership workshops, programmes and retreats, as well as executive coaching for a limited number of senior leaders.

A gender-equity champion, Jess has a passion for working in the "Women in Leadership" space. An international, sought after keynote speaker, she is available to speak at your next event.

See www.jessstuart.co.nz for more details.

LEADERZEN PROGRAMME

Self mastery & mental fitness for calm, conscious, capable leaders

Available in-house for your leadership team with in-person and online delivery options.

This unique programme includes:

- Three bespoke leadership workshops
- Monthly follow up coaching and support
- Additional resources, reading material and online learning to support implementation
- Tailoring to an organisation's needs, not off-the-shelf
- Shared learning and understanding; leadership teams talking the same language
- Practical strategies and proven experience, tried and tested in the leadership world

LeaderZEN helps educate leaders to:

- Leverage self mastery and awareness as core leadership skills
- Develop an ability to adapt to change effortlessly and bounce back from setbacks
- Increase focus and concentration, and access a flow state to enhance productivity
- Become fearless but wise, compassionate and respected
- Be empathic, with the ability to regulate and control emotional response

- Be an energised sustainable resource with the ability to innovate
- Embrace trust and presence of mind to guide both decision making and conflict resolution
- Develop mental fitness and perform at your peak

Develop the kind of calm that is contagious: when you speak, others listen. As a conscious leader, you know who you are and stand in your power; cognisant and composed to navigate the challenges ahead and make an impact.

ABOUT THE AUTHOR

Jess Stuart is a prolific author, executive coach and international speaker who empowers people to be their best without burning out in the process.

A highly acclaimed event speaker, Jess has been featured on TV3, the BBC, Radio New Zealand, Stuff, Tiny Buddha, Elephant Journal, and in the Dominion Post and NZ Business Magazine.

With a background in senior HR roles and a decade in the corporate world, Jess has been a senior leader herself and coached hundreds of others.

She helps busy high achievers to find more time, reprioritise what matters, build resilience, beat the overwhelm, keep calm in the chaos, realise their potential and develop the art of self mastery.

A brush with burnout in her corporate career led Jess across the world to train with Buddhist monks and nuns. A decade later, after coming out, writing six books and running her own successful business, she shares what she knows about leadership, mindset, resilience and self-belief to empower people to unlock their potential.

Born in Leicestershire, England, Jess now lives on Waiheke Island, New Zealand, with her wife and their dog Minnie. Outside of work, she'll be found at the beach, on road trips, surfing, close to nature and the ocean, or sitting quietly in the sun. A daily yoga and meditation practice keeps her grounded and gives her the energy for the work she loves. Regular trips back to spend time with family in the UK are a must for Jess, who considers herself a Kiwi now.

www.ingramcontent.com/pod-product-compliance
Lightning Source LLC
Chambersburg PA
CBHW061543050726

47593CB00002B/889